LITERARY STYLE AND MUSIC

LITERARY STYLE AND MUSIC

Including Two Short Essays on Gracefulness and Beauty

BY

HERBERT SPENCER

KENNIKAT PRESS
Port Washington, N. Y./London

LITERARY STYLE AND MUSIC

Published, 1951, by Philosophical Library, Inc.
Reissued in 1970 by Kennikat Press by arrangement
Library of Congress Catalog Card No: 78-91057
SBN 3046-0667-6

Manufactured by Taylor Publishing Company   Dallas, Texas

CONTENTS

INTRODUCTION

By CHARLES T. SMITH

THERE is usually a period in the early life of the great philosopher during which he produces works that represent a stropping of the mind to give it edge for fashioning prospective masterpieces. These essays are the product of such a period in Spencer's life. In composing them Spencer was able to test the keenness of his mental equipment. That he was satisfied with the results there can be no doubt; for he re-issued the essays in book form, he kept up a running defence of them against a succession of attacks, and in his last book, *Facts and Comments*, published only a year before his death, he fortified his doctrines with fresh arguments and with additional dissertations on kindred themes.

The first essay was prompted by an incident that induced Spencer to inquire why certain words and allocations of words are more effective than others. In view of the title of the essay, he was blamed for dealing only with " the backbone of the subject " and ignoring those traits of style which give quality, distinction, and colour. Spencer replied that his essay never purported to be more than the outcome of the limited inquiry he had been urged to undertake, and that its original title was " Force of Expression." It was submitted to the editor of *Fraser's Magazine*, and rejected. Ten years later, in its present improved form, it was published in *The Westminster Review*, the editor being responsible for its new and somewhat misleading title. Later in life Spencer commented on his own style of writing and, mindful of his earlier advocacy of the use of short Anglo-Saxon words, says he was surprised to find, on looking through *First Principles*, the introductory volume to his Synthetic Philosophy, how frequently he had employed words of Latin and Greek extraction. He suggests that this was probably owing to the fact that he was dealing with abstract and general ideas, for the expression of which the Anglo-Saxon vocabulary is deficient. He admits, however, that there were some words of native origin which he could have used. When revising the work he applied his strictures on style, and by cutting out superfluous words, clauses, sentences, and sometimes paragraphs, he was able to abridge it by fifty pages—about one-tenth. He did not think a *genuine* style could be acquired; he thought it was organic—a constituent of personality; but he believed that its texture could be modified.

The essay on music won a permanent place in musical literature, but it aroused acute controversy. The reader will see how Spencer dealt with the countertheory of Darwin and the objections of Edmund Gurney. In *Facts and Comments* he replied to further objections in an equally trenchant manner, asserting that they concerned the evolution and growth of music, not its origin. In order not to be misunderstood he added an essay in which he indicated the scope of a " theory of music at large," covering the whole ground.

The speech theory of the origin of music has had considerable vogue and has often been accepted as an æsthetic fact. Wagner, working along his own lines, apparently subscribed to it, and this led Ernest Newman, in *A Study of Wagner*, to take the opportunity of questioning its validity. Spencer conceded the cleverness of the criticism and, to his own satisfaction, rebutted it. Newman then developed a brilliant onslaught in *Musical Studies*, published in 1905, two years after Spencer's death. Had Spencer lived to reply, there would have been a battle royal—and no armistice.

Newman's attack, supported by arguments as cogent as those of his opponent, is impressive. Against the speech theory Newman maintained that music is a natural language in its own right and that it never needed to pass through the intermediate stage of imitation or exaggeration of the accents of speech. He claimed that in primitive man there is a real musical sense independent of speech and probably earlier in order of time. This musical sense, Newman contended, gives rise to what Jules Combarieu described as " thinking with sounds," as distinct from " thinking with words," the difference being one of *kind*, not of *degree*. Why music exhibits some of the traits of speech is because music and speech are the expression of allied modes of feeling, and are vented through the same muscular apparatus. Newman surmised that instead of being derived one from the other, they could both have emerged from certain causal phenomena which they have in common. The dispute concerning the origin of music is still unsettled, for no one has yet said the last word.

The two shorter essays are further examples of Spencer's powers of discerning and interpreting, with patient and scrupulous accuracy, the basic elements of æsthetics.

The feature that links the four essays and also gives them lasting value is the attitude of mind they exemplify. This attitude is evident in Spencer's method of starting from the simple indisputable facts of man's physiological and psychological make-up and then construing his arguments in accordance with the " law of parsimony "—a law in logic forbidding us to seek remote explanations of facts when close-at-hand explanations are sufficient. Hence there is no reliance on the credulities of fancy, or mystery, or mysticism; no indulgence in abstractions or in metaphysical dialectics; no traffic with supernaturalism. The scientific mind is seen operating in a scientific way and ensuring that the essays shall all bear the stamp of clear, direct, unemotional thinking. The method of approach, pursued with intellectual integrity—and that is what ultimately matters in the search for truth— carried conviction, the more so because it was a procedure from which Spencer never consciously deviated.

The instructive character of the related causes and effects which Spencer cites is also noteworthy. They make it quite clear that our most elemental (and, in a sense, most profound) emotional responses are derived from deep-rooted physiological reactions which conform to natural laws, and that in consequence a work of art will not evoke such responses unless it is designed in compliance with these laws. In demonstrating that the successful effects of artistic expression are therefore firmly pre-conditioned by forces to which the powers of genius and inspiration must submit, Spencer made a significant contribution to our understanding of æsthetic appeals.

Much of what Spencer wrote has since been incorporated in more comprehensive studies, but these are not readily available in popular form. Moreover, some of them are marred by abstruse speculations and by æsthetics being given a theological context. Spencer's essays are devoid of all such defects and can be appreciated as a sound introduction to the very contentious subjects with which they deal.

December, 1949.

THE PHILOSOPHY OF STYLE

[*First published in* The Westminster Review *for October* 1852.]

COMMENTING on the seeming incongruity between his father's argumentative powers and his ignorance of formal logic, Tristram Shandy says: " It was a matter of just wonder with my worthy tutor and two or three fellows of that learned society that a man who knew not so much as the names of his tools should be able to work after that fashion with them." Sterne's implied conclusion that a knowledge of the principles of reasoning neither makes, nor is essential to, a good reasoner is doubtless true. Thus, too, is it with grammar. As Dr. Latham, condemning the usual school-drill in Lindley Murray, rightly remarks: " Gross vulgarity is a fault to be prevented; but the proper prevention is to be got from habit—not rules." Similarly, good composition is far less dependent on acquaintance with its laws than on practice and natural aptitude. A clear head, a quick imagination, and a sensitive ear will go far towards making all rhetorical precepts needless. And where there exists any mental flaw—where there is a deficient verbal memory, or an inadequate sense of logical dependence, or but little perception of order, or a lack of constructive ingenuity—no amount of instruction will insure good writing. Nevertheless *some* results may be expected from a familiarity with the principles of style. The endeavour to conform to laws may tell, though slowly. And if in no other way, yet, as facilitating revision, a knowledge of the thing to be achieved—a clear idea of what constitutes a beauty and what a blemish—cannot fail to be of service.

No general theory of expression seems yet to have been enunciated. The maxims contained in works on composition and rhetoric are presented in an unorganized form. Standing as isolated dogmas—as empirical generalizations—they are neither so clearly apprehended nor so much respected as they would be were they deduced from some simple first principle. We are told that " brevity is the soul of wit." We hear styles condemned as verbose or involved. Blair says that every needless part of a sentence " interrupts the description and clogs the image "; and again, that " long sentences fatigue the reader's attention." It is remarked by Lord Kaimes that " to give the utmost force to a period it ought, if possible, to be closed with the word that makes the greatest figure." Avoidance of parentheses, and the use of Saxon words in preference to those of Latin origin, are often insisted upon. But, however influential the precepts thus dogmatically expressed, they would be much more influential if reduced to something like scientific ordination. In this, as in other cases, conviction is strengthened when we understand the *why*. And we may be sure that recognition of the general principle from which the rules of composition result will not only bring them home to us with greater force, but will disclose other rules of like origin.

On seeking for some clue to the law underlying these current maxims, we may see implied in many of them the importance of economizing the reader's or hearer's attention. To so present ideas that they may be apprehended with the least possible mental effort is the desideratum towards which most of the rules above quoted point. When we condemn writing that is wordy, or confused, or intricate; when we praise this style as easy and blame that as fatiguing, we consciously or unconsciously assume this desideratum as our standard of judgment. Regarding language as an apparatus of symbols for conveying thought, we may say that, as in a mechanical apparatus, the more simple and the better arranged its parts, the greater will be the effect produced. In either case, whatever force is absorbed by the machine is deducted from the result. A reader or listener has at each moment but a limited amount of mental power available. To recognize and interpret the symbols presented to him requires part of this power; to arrange and combine the images suggested by them requires a further part; and only that part which remains can be used for framing the thought expressed. Hence the more time and attention it takes to receive and understand each sentence, the less time and attention can be given to the contained idea, and the less vividly will that idea be conceived. How truly language must be regarded as a hindrance to thought, though the necessary instrument of it, we shall clearly perceive on remembering the comparative force with which simple ideas are communicated by signs. To say " Leave the room " is less expressive than to point to the door. Placing a finger on the lips is more forcible than whispering " Do not speak." A beck of the hand is better than " Come here." No phrase can convey the idea of surprise so vividly as opening the eyes and raising the eyebrows.

A shrug of the shoulders would lose much by transla-
tion into words. Again, it may be remarked that
when oral language is employed, the strongest effects
are produced by interjections, which condense entire
sentences into syllables. And in other cases, where
custom allows us to express thoughts by single words,
as in "beware," "heigho," "fudge," much force
would be lost by expanding them into specific propositions. Hence, carrying out the metaphor that
language is the vehicle of thought, we may say that in
all cases the friction and inertia of the vehicle deduct
from its efficiency, and that in composition the chief
thing to be done is to reduce the friction and inertia to
the smallest amounts. Let us then inquire whether
economy of the recipient's attention is not the secret
of effect, alike in the right choice and collocation of
words, in the best arrangement of clauses in a sentence, in the proper order of its principal and subordinate propositions, in the judicious use of simile,
metaphor, and other figures of speech, and even in the
rhythmical sequence of syllables.

The greater forcibleness of Saxon English, or rather
non-Latin English, first claims our attention. The
several special reasons assignable for this may all be
reduced to the general reason—economy. The most
important of them is early association. A child's
vocabulary is almost wholly Saxon. He says "I
have," not "I possess"; "I wish," not "I desire";
he does not "reflect," he "thinks"; he does not beg
for "amusement," but for "play"; he calls things
"nice" or "nasty," not "pleasant" or "disagreeable."
The synonyms learned in after years never become so
closely, so organically, connected with the ideas

signified as do these original words used in childhood; the association remains less strong. But in what does a strong association between a word and an idea differ from a weak one? Essentially in the greater ease and rapidity of the suggestive action. Both of two words, if they be strictly synonymous, eventually call up the same image. The expression " It is *acid*" must in the end give rise to the same thought as " It is *sour* "; but because the term " acid " was learnt later in life, and has not been so often followed by the ideal sensation symbolized, it does not so readily arouse that ideal sensation as the term " sour." If we remember how slowly the meanings follow unfamiliar words in another language, and how increasing familiarity with them brings greater rapidity and ease of comprehension; and if we consider that the like effect must have resulted from using the words of our mother-tongue from childhood upwards; we shall clearly see that the earliest learnt and oftenest used words will, other things equal, call up images with less loss of time and energy than their later learnt equivalents.

The further superiority possessed by Saxon English in its comparative brevity obviously comes under the same generalization. If it be an advantage to express an idea in the smallest number of words, then it must be an advantage to express it in the smallest number of syllables. If circuitous phrases and needless expletives distract the attention and diminish the strength of the impression produced, then so, too, must surplus articulations. A certain effort, though commonly an inappreciable one, is required to recognize every vowel and consonant. If, as all know, it is tiresome to listen to an indistinct speaker, or to read an ill-written manuscript; and if, as we cannot doubt, the fatigue is a cumulative result of the attention needed to catch successive syllables; it follows that attention is in such cases absorbed by each syllable. And this being so when the syllables are difficult of recognition, it will be so too, though in a less degree, when the recognition of them is easy. Hence, the shortness of Saxon words becomes a reason for their greater force. One qualification, however, must not be overlooked. A word which embodies the most important part of the idea to be conveyed, especially when emotion is to be produced, may often with advantage be a polysyllabic word. Thus it seems more forcible to say " It is *magnificent* " than " It is *grand*." The word " vast " is not so powerful a one as " stupendous." Calling a thing " nasty " is not so effective as calling it " disgusting." There seem to be several causes for this exceptional superiority of certain long words. We may ascribe it partly to the fact that a voluminous, mouth-filling epithet is, by its very size, suggestive of largeness or strength, as is shown by the pomposity of sesquipedalian verbiage; and when great power or intensity has to be suggested, this association of ideas aids the effect. A further cause may be that a word of several syllables admits of more emphatic articulation; and as emphatic articulation is a sign of emotion, the unusual impressiveness of the thing named is implied by it. Yet another cause is that a long word (of which the latter syllables are generally inferred as soon as the first are spoken) allows the hearer's consciousness more time to dwell on the quality predicated; and where, as in the above cases, it is to this predicated quality that the entire attention is called, an advantage results from keeping it before the mind for an appreciable interval. To make our generalization quite correct we must therefore say, that while in certain sentences expressing feeling, the word which more especially implies that feeling may often with advantage be a many-syllabled one; in the immense majority of cases each word, serving but as a step to the idea embodied by the whole sentence, should, if possible, be a single syllable.

Once more, that frequent cause of strength in Saxon and other primitive words—their onomatopœia—may be similarly resolved into the more general cause. Both those directly imitative, as " splash," " bang," " whiz," " roar," etc., and those analogically imitative, as " rough," " smooth," " keen," " blunt," " thin," " hard," " crag," etc., have a greater or less likeness to the things symbolized; and, by making on the ears impressions allied to the ideas to be called up, they save part of the effort needed to call up such ideas and leave more attention for the ideas themselves.

Economy of the recipient's mental energy may be assigned, too, as a manifest cause for the superiority of specific over generic words. That concrete terms produce more vivid impressions than abstract ones, and should, when possible, be used instead, is a current maxim of composition. As Dr. Campbell says: " The more general the terms are, the picture is the fainter; the more special they are, the brighter." When aiming at effect we should avoid such a sentence as :—

When the manners, customs, and amusements of a nation are cruel and barbarous, the regulations of their penal code will be severe.

B

And in place of it we should write:—

> When men delight in battles, bull-fights, and combats of gladiators, will they punish by hanging, burning, and the rack.

This superiority of specific expressions is clearly due to a saving of the effort required to translate words into thoughts. As we do not think in generals but in particulars—as, whenever any class of things is named, we represent it to ourselves by calling to mind individual members of the class—it follows that when a general word is used the hearer or reader has to choose from his stock of images, one or more, by which he may figure to himself the whole group. In doing this, some delay must arise—some force be expended; and if, by employing a specific term, an appropriate image can be at once suggested, an economy is achieved and a more vivid impression produced.

Turning now from the choice of words to their sequence, we find the same principle holds good. We have *a priori* reasons for believing that there is some one order of words by which every proposition may be more effectively expressed than by any other, and that this order is the one which presents the elements of the proposition in the succession in which they may be most readily put together. As in a narrative, the events should be stated in such sequence that the mind may not have to go backwards and forwards in order to rightly connect them; as in a group of sentences, the arrangement should be such that each of them may be understood as it comes, without waiting for subsequent ones; so, in every sentence, the sequence of words should be that which suggests the constituents of the thought in the order most convenient for building it up. Duly to enforce this truth, and to prepare the way for applications of it, we must analyse the mental act by which the meaning of a series of words is apprehended.

We cannot more simply do this than by considering the proper collocation of substantive and adjective. Is it better to place the adjective before the substantive, or the substantive before the adjective? Ought we to say, with the French, " un cheval noir "; or to say, as we do, " a black horse "? Probably most persons of culture will say that one order is as good as the other. Alive to the bias produced by habit, they will ascribe to that the preference they feel for our own form of expression. They will expect those educated in the use of the opposite form to have an equal preference for that. And thus they will conclude that neither of these instinctive judgments is of any worth. There is, however, a psychological ground for deciding in favour of the English custom. If " a horse black " be the arrangement, then immediately on the utterance of the word " horse " there arises, or tends to arise, in the mind an idea answering to that word; and as there has been nothing to indicate what *kind* of horse, any image of a horse suggests itself. Very likely, however, the image will be that of a brown horse, brown horses being the most familiar. The result is that when the word " black " is added a check is given to the process of thought. Either the picture of a brown horse already present to the imagination has to be suppressed and the picture of a black one summoned in its place, or else, if the picture of a brown horse be yet unformed, the tendency to form it has to be stopped.

Whichever is the case, some hindrance results. But if on the other hand " a black horse " be the expression used, no mistake can be made. The word " black," indicating an abstract quality, arouses no definite idea. It simply prepares the mind for conceiving some object of that colour, and the attention is kept suspended until that object is known. If, then, by precedence of the adjective the idea is always conveyed rightly, whereas precedence of the substantive is apt to produce a misconception, it follows that the one gives the mind less trouble than the other and is therefore more forcible.

Possibly it will be objected that the adjective and substantive come so close together that practically they may be considered as uttered at the same moment, and that on hearing the phrase, " a horse black," there is not time to imagine a wrongly coloured horse before the word " black " follows to prevent it. It must be owned that it is not easy to decide by introspection whether this is so or not. But there are facts collaterally implying that it is not. Our ability to anticipate the words yet unspoken is one of them. If the ideas of the hearer lingered behind the expressions of the speaker, as the objection assumes, he could hardly foresee the end of a sentence by the time it was half delivered; yet this constantly happens. Were the supposition true, the mind, instead of anticipating, would fall more and more in arrear. If the meanings of words are not realized as fast as the words are uttered, then the loss of time over each word must entail an accumulation of delays and leave a hearer entirely behind. But whether the force of these replies be or be not admitted, it will scarcely be denied that the right formation of a picture must be facilitated by presenting its elements in the order in which they are wanted, even though the mind should do nothing until it has received them all.

What is here said respecting the succession of the adjective and substantive is applicable, by change of terms, to the adverb and verb. And without further explanation it will be manifest that in the use of pre-positions and other particles most languages spon-taneously conform with more or less completeness to this law.

On similarly analysing sentences considered as vehicles for entire propositions, we find not only that the same principle holds good, but that the advantage of respecting it becomes marked. In the arrangement of predicate and subject, for example, we are at once shown that as the predicate determines the aspect under which the subject is to be conceived, it should be placed first; and the striking effect produced by so placing it becomes comprehensible. Take the often-quoted contrast between " Great is Diana of the Ephesians," and " Diana of the Ephesians is great." When the first arrangement is used, the utterance of the word " great," arousing vague associations of an imposing nature, prepares the imagination to clothe with high attributes whatever follows; and when the words " Diana of the Ephesians " are heard, appro-priate imagery, already nascent in thought, is used in the formation of the picture, the mind being thus led directly and without error to the intended impression. But when the reverse order is followed, the idea " Diana of the Ephesians " is formed with no special reference to greatness; and when the words " is great " are added, it has to be formed afresh; whence arises a loss of mental energy and a corresponding diminution of effect. The following verse from Coleridge's *Ancient Mariner*, though incomplete as a sentence, well illustrates the same truth:—

> *Alone, alone, all, all alone,*
> *Alone on a wide wide sea!*
> And never a saint took pity on
> My soul in agony.

Of course the principle equally applies when the predicate is a verb or a participle. And as effect is gained by placing first all words indicating the quality, conduct, or condition of the subject, it follows that the copula also should have precedence. It is true that the general habit of our language resists this arrangement of predicate, copula, and subject, but we may readily find instances of the additional force gained by conforming to it. Thus in the line from *Julius Cæsar*—

> Then *burst* his mighty heart,

priority is given to a word embodying both predicate and copula. In a passage contained in Sir W. Scott's *Marmion*, the like order is systematically employed with great effect:—

> The Border slogan rent the sky!
> *A Home! a Gordon! was* the cry;
> *Loud were* the clanging blows;
> *Advanced,—forced back,—now low, now high,*
>   The pennon sunk and rose;
> As *bends* the bark's mast in the gale
> When *rent are* rigging, shrouds, and sail,
>   It waver'd 'mid the foes.

Pursuing the principle further, it is obvious that, for producing the greatest effect, not only should the main divisions of a sentence observe this sequence, but the subdivisions of these should have their parts similarly arranged. In nearly all cases the predicate is accompanied by some limit or qualification called its complement. Commonly, also, the circumstances of the subject, which form its complement, have to be specified. And as these qualifications and circumstances must determine the mode in which the acts and things they belong to are conceived, precedence should be given to them. Lord Kaimes notices the fact that this order is preferable, though without giving the reason. He says: " When a circumstance is placed at the beginning of the period, or near the beginning, the transition from it to the principal subject is agreeable: is like ascending or going upward." A sentence arranged in illustration of this will be desirable. Here is one:—

> Whatever it may be in theory, it is clear that in practice the French idea of liberty is the right of every man to be master of the rest.

In this case, were the first two clauses, up to the word " practice " inclusive, which qualify the subject, to be placed at the end instead of the beginning, much of the force would be lost; as thus:—

> The French idea of liberty is the right of every man to be master of the rest; in practice at least, if not in theory.

Similarly with respect to the conditions under which any fact is predicated. Observe in the following example the effect of putting them last:—

> How immense would be the stimulus to progress were the honour now given to wealth and title given exclusively to high achievements and intrinsic worth!

And then observe the superior effect of putting them first :—

> Were the honour now given to wealth and title given exclusively to high achievements and intrinsic worth, how immense would be the stimulus to progress!

The effect of giving priority to the complement of the predicate, as well as the predicate itself, is finely displayed in the opening of *Hyperion :*—

> *Deep in the shady sadness of a vale*
> *Far sunken from the healthy breath of morn,*
> *Far from the fiery noon, and eve's one star,*
> *Sat* grey-haired Saturn, quiet as a stone.

Here we see not only that the predicate " sat " precedes the subject " Saturn," and that the three lines in italics, constituting the complement of the predicate, come before it, but that in the structure of this complement also, the same order is followed: each line being so composed that the qualifying words are placed before the words suggesting concrete images.

The right succession of the principal and subordinate propositions in a sentence depends on the same law. Regard for economy of the recipient's attention, which, as we find, determines the best order for the subject, copula, predicate, and their complements, dictates that the subordinate proposition shall precede the principal one when the sentence includes two. Containing, as the subordinate proposition does, some qualifying or explanatory idea, its priority prevents misconception of the principal one, and therefore saves the mental effort needed to correct such misconception.   This will be seen in the annexed example:—

> The secrecy once maintained in respect to the parliamentary debates is still thought needful in diplomacy; and diplomacy being secret, England may any day be unawares betrayed by its ministers into a war costing a hundred thousand lives, and hundreds of millions of treasure: yet the English pique themselves on being a self-governed people.

The two subordinate propositions, ending with the semicolon and colon respectively, almost wholly determine the meaning of the principal proposition with which the sentence concludes; and the effect would be lost were they placed last instead of first.

From this general principle of right arrangement may also be inferred the proper order of those minor divisions into which the major divisions of sentences may be decomposed.   In every sentence of any complexity the complement to the subject contains several clauses, and that to the predicate several others; and these may be arranged in greater or less conformity to the law of easy apprehension.   Of course with these, as with the larger members, the succession should be from the less specific to the more specific—from the abstract to the concrete.

Now, however, we must notice a further condition to be fulfilled in the proper construction of a sentence, but still a condition dictated by the same general principle with the other: the condition, namely, that the words or the expressions which refer to the most nearly connected thoughts shall be brought the closest together.   Evidently the single words, the minor clauses, and the leading divisions of every proposition, severally qualify each other. The longer the time that elapses between the mention of any qualifying member and the member qualified, the longer must the mind be exerted in carrying forward the qualifying member ready for use. And the more numerous the qualifications to be simultaneously remembered and rightly applied, the greater will be the mental power expended and the smaller the effect produced. Hence, other things equal, force will be gained by so arranging the members of a sentence that these suspensions shall at any moment be the fewest in number; and shall also be of the shortest duration. The following is an instance of defective combination:—

> A modern newspaper-statement, though probably true, would be laughed at if quoted in a book as testimony; but the letter of a court gossip is thought good historical evidence, if written some centuries ago.

A re-arrangement of this in accordance with the principle indicated above will be found to increase the effect. Thus:—

> Though probably true, a modern newspaper-statement quoted in a book as testimony would be laughed at; but the letter of a court gossip, if written some centuries ago, is thought good historical evidence.

By making this change, some of the suspensions are avoided and others shortened, while there is less liability to produce premature conceptions. The passage quoted below from *Paradise Lost* affords a fine instance of a sentence well arranged; alike in the priority of the subordinate members, in the avoidance

of long and numerous suspensions, and in the corre-
spondence between the sequence of the clauses and
the sequence of the phenomena described—which, by
the way, is a further prerequisite to easy apprehension,
and therefore to effect.

> As when a prowling wolf,
> Whom hunger drives to seek new haunt for prey,
> Watching where shepherds pen their flocks at eve,
> In hurdled cotes amid the field secure,
> Leaps o'er the fence with ease into the fold:
> Or as a thief, bent to unhoard the cash
> Of some rich burgher, whose substantial doors,
> Cross-barr'd and bolted fast, fear no assault,
> In at the window climbs, or o'er the tiles:
> So clomb the first grand Thief into God's fold;
> So since into his Church lewd hirelings climb.

The habitual use of sentences in which all or most of
the descriptive and limiting elements precede those
described and limited, gives rise to what is called the
inverted style: a title which is, however, by no means
confined to this structure, but is often used where the
order of the words is simply unusual. A more appropriate title would be the *direct style*, as contrasted with
the other, or *indirect style* : the peculiarity of the one
being that it conveys each thought step by step with
little liability to error; and of the other, that it conveys each thought by a series of approximations
which successively correct the erroneous preconcep-
tions that have been raised.

The superiority of the direct over the indirect form
of sentence implied by the several conclusions above
drawn, must not, however, be affirmed without reser-
vation. Though up to a certain point it is well for
the qualifying clauses of a proposition to precede
those qualified; yet, as carrying forward each qualify-

ing clause costs some mental effort, it follows that when the number of them and the time they are carried become great, we reach a limit beyond which more is lost than is gained.   Other things equal, the arrangement should be such that no concrete image shall be suggested until the materials out of which it is to be framed have been presented.   And yet, as lately pointed out, other things equal, the fewer the materials to be held at once, and the shorter the distance they have to be borne, the better.   Hence in some cases it becomes a question whether most mental effort will be entailed by the many and long suspensions or by the correction of successive misconceptions.

This question may sometimes be decided by considering the capacity of the persons addressed.   A greater grasp of mind is required for the ready apprehension of thoughts expressed in the direct manner where the sentences are anywise intricate.   To recollect a number of preliminaries stated in elucidation of a coming idea, and to apply them all to the formation of it when suggested, demands a good memory and considerable power of concentration.   To one possessing these the direct method will mostly seem the best, while to one deficient in them it will seem the worst.   Just as it may cost a strong man less effort to carry a hundredweight from place to place at once than by a stone at a time; so to an active mind it may be easier to bear along all the qualifications of an idea, and at once rightly form it when named, than to first imperfectly conceive such idea and then carry back to it, one by one, the details and limitations afterwards mentioned.   While conversely, as for a boy the only possible mode of transferring a hundredweight is that of taking it in

portions; so, for a weak mind, the only possible mode
of forming a compound conception may be that of
building it up by carrying separately its several
parts.

That the indirect method—the method of conveying
the meaning by a series of approximations—is best
fitted for the uncultivated may indeed be inferred from
their habitual use of it. The form of expression
adopted by the savage, as in " Water, give me," is the
simplest type of this arrangement. In pleonasms,
which are comparatively prevalent among the un-
educated, the same essential structure is seen; as, for
instance, in " The men, they were there." Again, the
old possessive case, " The king, his crown," conforms
to the like order of thought. Moreover, the fact that
the indirect mode is called the natural one implies that
it is the one spontaneously employed by the common
people—that is, the one easiest for undisciplined
minds.

There are many cases, however, in which neither the
direct nor the indirect mode is the best, but in which
an intermediate mode is preferable to both. When
the number of circumstances and qualifications to be
included in the sentences is great, the judicious course
is neither to enumerate them all before introducing the
idea to which they belong, nor to put this idea first
and let it be remodelled to agree with the particulars
afterwards mentioned, but to do a little of each. It is
desirable to avoid so extremely indirect an arrangement as the following:—

> We came to our journey's end, at last, with no
> small difficulty, after much fatigue, through deep
> roads, and bad weather.

Yet to transform this into an entirely direct sentence would be unadvisable; as witness:—

> At last, with no small difficulty, after much fatigue, through deep roads, and bad weather, we came to our journey's end.

Dr. Whately, from whom we quote the first of these two arrangements, proposes this construction :—

> "At last, after much fatigue, through deep roads and bad weather, we came, with no small difficulty, to our journey's end."

Here by introducing the words " we came " a little earlier in the sentence, the labour of carrying forward so many particulars is diminished, and the subsequent qualification " with no small difficulty " entails an addition to the thought that is easily made. But a further improvement may be effected by putting the words " we came " still earlier; especially if at the same time the qualifications be rearranged in conformity with the principle already explained—that the more abstract elements of the thought should come before the more concrete. Observe the result of making these two changes:—

> At last, with no small difficulty, and after much fatigue, we came, through deep roads and bad weather, to our journey's end.

This reads with comparative smoothness—that is, with less hindrance from suspensions and reconstructions of thought.

It should be further remarked that even when addressing vigorous intellects the direct mode is unfit for communicating ideas of a complex or abstract character.   So long as the mind has not much to do, it may be well able to grasp all the preparatory clauses of a sentence and to use them effectively; but if some subtlety in the argument absorb the attention it may happen that the mind, doubly strained, will break down, and allow the elements of the thought to lapse into confusion.

Let us now pass to figures of speech.   In them we may equally discern the same general law of effect. Implied in rules given for the choice and right use of them we shall find the same fundamental requirement —economy of attention.   It is indeed chiefly because they so well subserve this requirement that figures of speech are employed.

Let us begin with the figure called Synecdoche. The advantage sometimes gained by putting a part for the whole is due to the more convenient, or more vivid, presentation of the idea.   If, instead of writing " a fleet of ten ships," we write " a fleet of ten *sail*," the picture of a group of vessels at sea is more readily suggested, and is so because the sails constitute the most conspicuous parts of vessels so circumstanced. To say " All *hands* to the pumps " is better than to say " All *men* to the pumps," as it calls up a picture of the men in the special attitude intended and so saves effort.   Bringing "*grey hairs* with sorrow to the grave " is another expression the effect of which has the same cause.

The effectiveness of Metonymy may be similarly accounted for.   " The low morality of *the bar* " is a phrase both more brief and significant than the literal one it stands for.   A belief in the ultimate supremacy of intelligence over brute force is conveyed in a more concrete form, and therefore more representable form, if we substitute *the pen* and *the sword* for the two abstract terms. To say " Beware of drinking! " is less effective than to say " Beware of *the bottle !* " and is so, clearly because it calls up a less specific image.

The Simile is in many cases used chiefly with a view to ornament; but whenever it increases the *force* of a passage, it does so by being an economy. Here is an instance:—

> The illusion that great men and great events came oftener in early times than they come now is due partly to historical perspective. As in a range of equidistant columns the furthest off seem the closest, so the conspicuous objects of the past seem more thickly clustered the more remote they are.

To express literally the thought thus conveyed would take many sentences, and the first elements of the picture would become faint while the imagination was busy in adding the others. But by the help of a comparison much of the effort otherwise required is saved.

Concerning the position of the Simile,[1] it needs only to remark that what has been said about the order of the adjective and substantive, predicate and subject, principal and subordinate propositions, etc., is applicable here. As whatever qualifies should precede

[1] Properly the term " simile " is applicable only to the entire figure, including the two things compared and the comparison drawn between them. But as there exists no name for the illustrative member of the figure, there seems no alternative but to employ " simile " to express this also. The context will in each case show in which sense the word is used.

whatever is qualified, force will generally be gained by placing the simile before the object or act to which it is applied. That this arrangement is the best may be seen in the following passage from the *Lady of the Lake* :—

> As wreath of snow, on mountain breast,
> Slides from the rock that gave it rest,
> Poor Ellen glided from her stay,
> And at the monarch's feet she lay.

Inverting these couplets will be found to diminish the effect considerably. There are cases, however, even where the simile is a simple one, in which it may with advantage be placed last; as in these lines from Alexander Smith's *Life Drama* :—

> I see the future stretch
> All dark and barren as a rainy sea.

The reason for this seems to be, that so abstract an idea as that attaching to the word " future " does not present itself to the mind in any definite form, and hence the subsequent arrival at the simile entails no reconstruction of the thought.

Such, however, are not the only cases in which this order is the more forcible. As putting the simile first is advantageous only when it is carried forward in the mind to assist in forming an image of the object or act; it must happen that if, from length or complexity, it cannot be so carried forward, the advantage is not gained. The annexed sonnet by Coleridge is defective from this cause :—

> As when a child, on some long winter's night,
> Affrighted, clinging to its grandam's knees,
> With eager wond'ring and perturb'd delight
> Listens strange tales of fearful dark decrees,

C

> Mutter'd to wretch by necromantic spell;
> Or of those hags who at the witching time
> Of murky midnight, ride the air sublime,
> And mingle foul embrace with fiends of hell;
> Cold horror drinks its blood! Anon the tear
> More gentle starts, to hear the beldame tell
> Of pretty babes, that lov'd each other dear,
> Murder'd by cruel uncle's mandate fell:
> Ev'n such the shiv'ring joys thy tones impart,
> Ev'n so, thou, Siddons, meltest my sad heart.

Here, from the lapse of time and accumulation of circumstances, the first member of the comparison is forgotten before the second is reached, and requires re-reading. Had the main idea been first mentioned, less effort would have been required to retain it, and to modify the conception of it into harmony with the illustrative ideas, than to remember the illustrative ideas and refer back to them for help in forming the final image.

The superiority of the Metaphor to the Simile is ascribed by Dr. Whately to the fact that " all men are more gratified at catching the resemblance for themselves, than in having it pointed out to them." But after what has been said, the great economy it achieves will seem the more probable cause. Lear's exclamation,

> Ingratitude! thou marble-hearted fiend,

would lose part of its effect were it changed into

> Ingratitude! thou fiend with heart like marble;

and the loss would result partly from the position of the simile and partly from the extra number of words required. When the comparison is an involved one, the greater force of the metaphor, due to its relative brevity, becomes much more conspicuous. If, drawing an analogy between mental and physical phenomena, we say,

> As, in passing through a crystal, beams of white light are decomposed into the colours of the rainbow, so, in traversing the soul of the poet, the colourless rays of truth are transformed into brightly-tinted poetry,

it is clear that in receiving the two sets of words expressing the two halves of the comparison, and in carrying the meaning of the one to help in interpreting the other, considerable attention is absorbed. Most of this is saved by putting the comparison in a metaphorical form, thus:—

> The white light of truth, in traversing the many-sided transparent soul of the poet, is refracted into iris-hued poetry.

How much is conveyed in a few words by using Metaphor, and how vivid the effect consequently produced, is everywhere shown. From *A Life Drama* may be quoted the phrase,

> I spear'd him with a jest,

as a fine instance among the many which that poem contains. A passage in the *Prometheus Unbound*, of Shelley, displays the power of the metaphor to great advantage:—

> Methought among the lawns together
> We wandered, underneath the young gray dawn,
> And multitudes of dense white fleecy clouds
> Were wandering in thick flocks along the mountains
> *Shepherded* by the slow unwilling wind.

This last expression is remarkable for the distinctness

with which it calls up the features of the scene, bringing the mind by a bound to the desired conception.

But a limit is put to the advantageous use of Metaphor by the condition that it must be simple enough to be understood from a hint. Evidently, if there be any obscurity in the meaning or application of it, no economy of attention will be achieved, but rather the reverse. Hence, when the comparison is complex, it is better to put it in the form of a Simile. There is, however, a species of figure, sometimes classed under Allegory, but which might well be called Compound Metaphor, that enables us to retain the brevity of the metaphorical form even where the analogy is intricate. This is done by indicating the application of the figure at the outset, and then leaving the reader or hearer to continue the parallel. Emerson has employed it with great effect in the first of his *Lectures on the Times* :—

> The main interest which any aspects of the Times can have for us, is the great spirit which gazes through them, the light which they can shed on the wonderful questions, What are we? and Whither do we tend? We do not wish to be deceived. Here we drift, like white sail across the wild ocean, now bright on the wave, now darkling in the trough of the sea; but from what port did we sail? Who knows? Or to what port are we bound? Who knows? There is no one to tell us but such poor weather-tossed mariners as ourselves, whom we speak as we pass, or who have hoisted some signal, or floated to us some letter in a bottle from afar. But what know they more than we? They also found themselves on this wondrous sea. No; from the older sailors

nothing. Over all their speaking-trumpets the
gray sea and the loud winds answer—Not in us;
not in Time.

The division of Simile from Metaphor is by no means
definite. Between the one extreme in which the two
elements of the comparison are detailed at full length
and the analogy pointed out, and the other extreme in
which the comparison is implied instead of stated,
come intermediate forms, in which the comparison is
partly stated and partly implied. For instance:—

Astonished at the performances of the English
plough, the Hindoos paint it, set it up, and worship
it, thus turning a tool into an idol. Linguists do
the same with language.

Here there is an evident advantage in leaving the
reader or hearer to complete the figure. And generally these intermediate forms are good in proportion
as they do this, provided the mode of completion be
obvious.

Passing over much that may be said of like purport
on Hyperbole, Personification, Apostrophe, etc., let us
close our remarks on construction by a typical example
of effective expression. The general principle which
has been enunciated is that, other things equal, the force
of a verbal form or arrangement is great in proportion
as the mental effort demanded from the recipient is
small. The corollaries from this general principle have
been severally illustrated. But though conformity
now to this and now to that requirement has been
exemplified, no case of entire conformity has yet been
quoted. It is indeed difficult to find one, for the
English idiom does not commonly permit the order

which theory dictates. A few, however, occur in Ossian. Here is one:—

> Like autumn's dark storms pouring from two echoing hills, towards each other approached the heroes. Like two deep streams from high rocks meeting, mixing, roaring on the plain; loud, rough, and dark in battle meet Lochlin and Inisfail. . . . As the noise of the troubled ocean when roll the waves on high; as the last peal of the thunder of heaven; such is the din of war.

Except in the position of the verb in the first two similes, the theoretically best arrangement is fully carried out in each of these sentences. The simile comes before the qualified image, the adjectives before the substantives, the predicate and copula before the subject, and their respective complements before them. That the passage is bombastic proves nothing; or rather, proves our case. For what is bombast but a force of expression too great for the magnitude of the ideas embodied? All that may rightly be inferred is that only in rare cases should *all* the conditions to effective expression be fulfilled.

A more complex application of the theory may now be made. Not only in the structures of sentences and the uses of figures of speech may we trace economy of the recipient's mental energy as the cause of force, but we may trace this same cause in the successful choice and arrangement of the minor images out of which some large thought is to be built. To select, from a scene or event described, those elements which carry many others with them, and so, by saying a few things but suggesting many, to abridge the description, is the

secret of producing a vivid impression. An extract
from Tennyson's *Mariana* will well illustrate this:—

> All day within the dreamy house,
> The doors upon their hinges creaked,
> The blue fly sung in the pane; the mouse
> Behind the mouldering wainscot shriek'd,
> Or from the crevice peer'd about.

The several circumstances here specified bring with
them many appropriate associations. When alone,
the creaking of a distant door is much more obtrusive
than when talking to friends. Our attention is rarely
drawn by the buzzing of a fly in the window save when
everything is still. While the inmates are moving
about the house, mice usually keep silence, and it is
only when extreme quietness reigns that they peep
from their retreats. Hence each of the facts mentioned, presupposing various others, calls up these
with more or less distinctness and revives the feeling
of dull solitude with which they are connected in our
experience. Were all of them detailed instead of
suggested, the mental energies would be so frittered
away in attending that little impression of dreariness
would be produced. Similarly in other cases. In the
choice of component ideas, as in the choice of expressions, the aim must be to convey the greatest
quantity of thoughts with the smallest quantity of
words.

The same principle may sometimes be advantageously
carried yet further by indirectly suggesting some
entirely distinct thought in addition to the one expressed. Thus if we say,

> The head of a good classic is as full of ancient
> myths as that of a servant-girl of ghost stories,

it is manifest that besides the fact asserted there is an
implied opinion respecting the small value of much that
passes as classical learning, and as this implied opinion
is recognized much sooner than it can be put into
words, there is gain in omitting it. In other cases,
again, great effect is produced by an overt omission,
provided the nature of the idea left out is obvious A
good instance occurs in *Heroes and Hero-worship*.
After describing the way in which Burns was sacrificed
to the idle curiosity of lion-hunters—people who
sought to amuse themselves, and who got their amusement while " the Hero's life went for it! "—Carlyle
suggests a parallel thus :—

> " Richter says, in the Island of Sumatra there
> is a kind of ' Light-chafers,' large Fire-flies, which
> people stick upon spits, and illuminate the ways
> with at night. Persons of condition can thus
> travel with a pleasant radiance, which they
> much admire. Great honour to the Fire-flies!
> But—!—"

Before inquiring whether the law of effect thus far
traced explains the impressiveness of poetry as compared with prose, it will be needful to notice some
causes of force in expression which have not yet been
mentioned. These are not, properly speaking, additional causes, but rather secondary ones, originating
from those already specified. One is that mental
excitement spontaneously prompts those forms of
speech which have been pointed out as the most
effective. " Out with him! " " Away with him! "
are the cries of angry citizens at a disturbed meeting.
A voyager, describing a terrible storm he had witnessed,

would rise to some such climax as: " Crack, went the ropes, and down came the mast." Astonishment may be heard expressed in the phrase, " Never was there such a sight! " All of which sentences are constructed after the direct type. Again, there is the fact that excited persons are given to figures of speech. The vituperation of the vulgar abounds with them. " Beast," " brute," " gallows rogue," " cut-throat villain "—these, and like metaphors or metaphorical epithets, call to mind a street quarrel. Further, it may be noticed that extreme brevity is a trait of passionate language. The sentences are generally incomplete, and frequently important words are left to be gathered from the context. Great admiration does not vent itself in a precise proposition, as, " It is beautiful," but in the simple exclamation, " Beautiful! " He who, when reading a lawyer's letter, should say " Vile rascal! " would be thought angry, while " He is a vile rascal " would imply comparative coolness. Thus alike in the order of the words, in the frequent use of figures, and in extreme conciseness, the natural utterances of excitement conform to the theoretical conditions to forcible expression.

Hence such forms of speech acquire a secondary strength from association. Having in daily intercourse heard them in connection with vivid mental impressions, and having been accustomed to meet with them in writing of unusual power, they come to have in themselves a species of force. The emotions that have from time to time been produced by the strong thoughts wrapped up in these forms are partially aroused by the forms themselves. These create a preparatory sympathy, and when the striking ideas looked for are reached, they are the more vividly pictured.

The continuous use of words and forms that are alike forcible in themselves and forcible from their associations produces the impressive species of composition which we call poetry. The poet habitually adopts those symbols of thought and those methods of using them which instinct and analysis agree in choosing as most effective. On turning back to the various specimens which have been quoted it will be seen that the direct or inverted form of sentence predominates in them, and that to a degree inadmissible in prose. Not only in the frequency, but in what is termed the violence of the inversions, may this distinction be remarked. The abundant use of figures, again, exhibits the same truth. Metaphors, similes, hyperboles, and personifications are the poet's colours, which he has liberty to employ almost without limit. We characterize as " poetical " the prose which uses these appliances of language with frequency, and condemn it as " over-florid " or " affected " long before they occur with the profusion allowed in verse. Once more, in brevity—the other requisite of forcible expression which theory points out and emotion spontaneously fulfils—poetical phraseology differs from ordinary phraseology. Imperfect periods are frequent, elisions are perpetual, and many minor words which would be deemed essential in prose are dispensed with.

Thus poetry is especially impressive partly because it conforms to all the laws of effective speech, and partly because in so doing it imitates the natural utterances of excitement. While the matter embodied is idealized emotion, the vehicle is the idealized language of emotion. As the musical composer catches the cadences in which our feelings of joy and sympathy, grief and despair, vent themselves, and out of these germs evolves melodies suggesting higher phases of these feelings; so the poet develops, from the typical expressions in which men utter passion and sentiment, those choice forms of verbal combination in which concentrated passion and sentiment may be fitly presented.

There is one peculiarity of poetry conducing much to its effect—the peculiarity which is indeed usually thought its characteristic one—still remaining to be considered: we mean its rhythmical structure. This, improbable though it seems, will be found to come under the same generalization with the others. Like each of them, it is an idealization of the natural language of emotion, which is not uncommonly more or less metrical if the emotion be not too violent; and like each of them it economizes the reader's or hearer's attention. In the peculiar tone and manner we adopt in uttering versified language may be discerned its relationship to the feelings, and the pleasure which its measured movement gives is ascribable to the comparative ease with which words metrically arranged can be recognized. This last position will not be at once admitted, but explanation will justify it. If, as we have seen, there is an expenditure of mental energy in so listening to verbal articulations as to identify the words, or in that silent repetition of them which goes on in reading, then any mode of so combining words as to present a regular recurrence of certain traits which can be anticipated will diminish that strain on the attention entailed by the total irregularity of prose. Just as the body, when receiving a series of varying concussions, must keep its muscles ready to meet the most violent of them, as not knowing when such may come; so the mind, when receiving unarranged articulations, must keep its perceptive faculties active enough to recognize the least easily caught sounds. And as, if the concussions recur in a definite order, the body may husband its forces by adjusting the resistance needful for each concussion; so, if the syllables be rhythmically arranged, the mind may economize its energies by anticipating the attention required for each syllable. Far-fetched though this idea will be thought, introspection countenances it. That we *do* take advantage of metrical language to adjust our perceptive faculties to the expected articutions is clear from the fact that we are balked by halting versification. Much as at the bottom of a flight of stairs a step more or less than we counted upon gives us a shock; so, too, does a misplaced accent or a supernumerary syllable. In the one case we *know* that there is an erroneous pre-adjustment, and we can scarcely doubt that there is one in the other. But if we habitually pre-adjust our perceptions to the measured movement of verse, the physical analogy above given renders it probable that by so doing we economize attention, and hence that metrical language is more effective than prose because it enables us to do this.

Were there space, it might be worth while to inquire whether the pleasure we take in rhyme, and also that which we take in euphony, are not partly ascribable to the same general cause.

A few paragraphs only can be devoted to a second

division of our subject. To pursue in detail the laws of effect as applying to the larger features of composition would carry us beyond our limits. But we may briefly indicate a further aspect of the general principle hitherto traced, and hint a few of its wider applications.

Thus far we have considered only those causes of force in language which depend on economy of the mental *energies*. We have now to glance at those which depend on economy of the mental *sensibilities*. Questionable though this division may be as a psychological one, it will serve roughly to indicate the remaining field of investigation. It will suggest that besides considering the extent to which any faculty or group of faculties is tasked in receiving a form of words and constructing its contained idea, we have to consider the state in which this faculty or group of faculties is left, and how the reception of subsequent sentences and images will be influenced by that state. Without going fully into so wide a topic as the action of faculties and its reactive effects, it will suffice to recall the fact that every faculty is exhausted by exercise. This generalization, which our bodily experiences force upon us and which in daily speech is recognized as true of the mind as a whole, is true of each mental power, from the simplest of the senses to the most complex of the sentiments. If we hold a flower to the nose for long we become insensible to its scent. We say of a brilliant flash of lightning that it blinds us; which means that our eyes have for a time lost their ability to appreciate light. After eating honey we are apt to think that our tea is without sugar. The phrase " a deafening roar " implies that men find a very loud sound temporarily incapacitates them for hearing faint sounds.   To a hand which has for some time carried a heavy body, small bodies afterwards lifted seem to have lost their weight.   Now, the truth thus exemplified may be traced throughout.   Alike of the reflective faculties, the imagination, the perceptions of the beautiful, the ludicrous, the sublime, it may be shown that action exhausts, and that in proportion as the action is violent the subsequent prostration is great.

Equally throughout the whole nature may be traced the law that exercised faculties are ever tending to resume their original states.   Not only after continued rest do they regain their full powers ; not only are brief cessations in the demands on them followed by partial re-invigoration; but even while they are in action the resulting exhaustion is ever being neutralized.   The processes of waste and repair go on together.   Hence with faculties habitually exercised—as the senses of all persons, or the muscles of any one who is strong—it happens that, during moderate activity, the repair is so nearly equal to the waste that the diminution of power is scarcely appreciable.   It is only when effort has been long continued, or has been violent, that repair becomes so far in arrear of waste as to cause a perceptible enfeeblement.   In all cases, however, when, by the action of a faculty, waste has been incurred, *some* lapse of time must take place before full efficiency can be re-acquired ; and this time must be long in proportion as the waste has been great.

Keeping in mind these general truths, we shall be in a condition to understand certain causes of effect in composition now to be considered.   Every perception received and every conception framed, entailing some amount of waste in the nervous system, and the efficiency of the faculties employed being for a time, though often but momentarily, diminished, the resulting partial inability affects the acts of perception and conception that immediately succeed. Hence the vividness with which images are pictured must, in many cases, depend on the order of their presentation, even when one order is as convenient to the understanding as the other. Sundry facts illustrate this truth and are explained by it: instance Climax and Anti-climax. The marked effect obtained by placing last the most striking of any series of ideas, and the weakness—often the ludicrous weakness—produced by reversing this arrangement, depends on the general law indicated. As immediately after looking at the sun we cannot perceive the light of a fire, while by looking at the fire first and the sun afterwards we can perceive both; so after receiving a brilliant, or weighty, or terrible thought, we cannot properly appreciate a less brilliant, less weighty, or less terrible one, though by reversing the order we can appreciate each. In Antithesis, again, the like truth is exemplified. The opposition of two thoughts which are the reverse of each other in some prominent trait insures an impressive effect, and does this by giving a momentary relaxation to the faculties addressed. If, after a series of ordinary images exciting in a moderate degree to the emotion of reverence, or approbation, or beauty, the mind has presented to it an insignificant, or unworthy, or ugly image, the structure which yields the emotion of reverence, or approbation, or beauty, having for the time nothing to do, tends to resume its full power, and will immediately afterwards appreciate anything vast, admirable, or beautiful better than it would otherwise do. Conversely, where the idea of absurdity due to extreme insignificance is to be produced, it may be intensified by placing it after something impressive, especially if the form of phrase implies that something still more impressive is coming. A good illustration of the effect gained by thus presenting a petty idea to a consciousness which has not yet recovered from the shock of an exciting one occurs in a sketch by Balzac. His hero writes to a mistress who has cooled towards him the following letter:—

> Madame,—Votre conduite m'étonne autant qu'elle m'afflige. Non contente de me déchirer le cœur par vos dédains, vous avez l'indélicatesse de me retenir une brosse à dents, que mes moyens ne me permettent pas de remplacer, mes propriétés étant greves d'hypothéques au delà de leur valeur.
> Adieu, trop belle et trop ingrate amie! Puissions-nous nous revoir dans un monde meilleur!
>
> CHARLES-EDOUARD.

Thus the phenomena of Climax, Antithesis, and Anti-climax, alike result from this general principle. Improbable as these momentary variations in susceptibility may seem, we cannot doubt their occurrence when we contemplate the analogous variations in the susceptibility of the senses. Every one knows that a patch of black on a white ground looks blacker, and a patch of white on a black ground looks whiter, than elsewhere. As the blackness and the whiteness are really the same, the only assignable cause is a difference in their actions upon us, dependent on the different states of our faculties. The effect is due to a visual anti-thesis.

But this extension of the general principle of economy—this further condition to effective composition, that the sensitiveness of the faculties must be husbanded—includes much more than has been yet hinted. Not only does it follow that certain arrangements and certain juxtapositions of connected ideas are best, but also that some modes of dividing and presenting a subject will be more striking than others, irrespective of logical cohesion. We are shown why we must progress from the less interesting to the more interesting, alike in the composition as a whole and in each successive portion. At the same time, the indicated requirement negatives long continuity of the same kind of thought, or repeated production of like effects. It warns us against the error committed by Pope in his poems and by Bacon in his essays—the error of constantly employing forcible forms of expression. As the easiest posture by and by becomes fatiguing, and is with pleasure exchanged for one less easy, so the most perfectly constructed sentences unceasingly used must cause weariness, and relief will be given by using those of inferior kinds. Further, we may infer not only that we ought to avoid generally combining our words in one manner, however good, or working out our figures and illustrations in one way, however telling, but that we ought to avoid anything like uniform adherence to the wider conditions of effect. We should not make every division of our subject progress in interest; we should not always rise to a climax. As we saw that in single sentences it is but rarely allowable to fulfil all the

D

conditions to strength, so in the larger sections of a composition we must not often conform entirely to the principles indicated. We must subordinate the component effects to the total effect.

The species of composition which the law we have traced out indicates as the perfect one is the one which genius tends naturally to produce. As we found that the kinds of sentence which are theoretically best are those commonly employed by superior minds, and by inferior minds when temporarily exalted, so we shall find that the ideal form for a poem, essay, or fiction is that which the ideal writer would evolve spontaneously. One in whom the powers of expression fully responded to the state of feeling would unconsciously use that variety in the mode of presenting his thoughts, which Art demands. Constant employment of one species of phraseology implies an undeveloped linguistic faculty. To have a specific style is to be poor in speech. If we remember that in the far past men had only nouns and verbs to convey their ideas with, and that from then to now the progress has been towards more numerous implements of thought and towards greater complexity and variety in their combinations, we may infer that in the use of sentences we are at present much what the primitive man was in the use of words, and that a continuance of the process which has hitherto gone on must produce increasing heterogeneity in our modes of expression. As now, in a fine nature, the play of the features, the tones of the voice and its cadences, vary in harmony with every thought uttered; so, in one possessed of fully developed powers of language, the mould in which each combination of words is cast will vary with, and be appropriate to, the mental state. That a perfectly endowed man must unconsciously write in all styles we may infer from considering how styles originate. Why is Johnson pompous, Goldsmith simple? Why is one author abrupt, another involved, another concise? Evidently in each case the habitual mode of utterance depends on the habitual balance of the nature. The dominant feelings have by use trained the intellect to represent them. But while long habit has made it do this efficiently, it remains, from lack of practice, unable to do the like for the less active feelings; and when these are excited the usual verbal forms undergo but slight modification. But let the ability of the intellect to represent the mental state be complete, and this fixity of style will disappear. The perfect writer will be now rhythmical and now irregular; here his language will be plain and there ornate; sometimes his sentences will be balanced and at other times unsymmetrical; for a while there will be considerable sameness and then again great variety. His mode of expression naturally responding to his thought and emotion, there will flow from his pen a composition changing as the aspects of his subject change. He will thus without effort conform to what we have seen to be the laws of effect. And while his work presents to the reader that variety needful to prevent continuous exertion of the same faculties, it will also answer to the description of all highly organized products both of man and nature. It will be, not a series of like parts simply placed in juxtaposition, but one whole made up of unlike parts that are mutually dependent.

POSTSCRIPT.—The conclusion that, because of their

comparative brevity and because of those stronger associations formed by more frequent use, words of Old-English origin are preferable to words derived from Latin or Greek should be taken with two qualifications, which it seems needful to add here.

In some cases the word furnished by our original tongue, and the corresponding word directly or indirectly derived from Latin, though nominally equivalents, are not actually such; and the word of Latin origin, by certain extra connotations it has acquired, may be the more expressive. For instance, we have no word of native origin which can be advantageously substituted for the word "grand." No such words as "big" or "great," which connote little more than superiority in size or quantity, can be used instead: they do not imply that qualitative superiority which is associated with the idea of grandeur. As adopted into our own language, the word "grand" has been differentiated from "great" by habitual use in those cases where the greatness has an æsthetic superiority. In this case, then, a word of Latin origin is better than its nearest equivalent of native origin, because by use it has acquired an additional meaning. And here, too, we may conveniently note the fact that the greater brevity of a word does not invariably conduce to greater force. Where the word, instead of being one conveying a subordinate component of the idea the sentence expresses, is one conveying the central element of the idea on which the attention may with advantage rest a moment, a longer word is sometimes better than a shorter word. Thus it may be held that the sentence "It is grand" is not so effective as the sentence "It is magnificent." Besides the fact that here greater length of the word favours a longer dwelling on the essential part of the thought, there is the fact that its greater length, aided by its division into syllables, gives opportunity for a cadence appropriate to the feeling produced by the thing characterized. By an ascent of the voice on the syllable " nif," and an utterance of this syllable, not only in a higher note, but with greater emphasis than the preceding or succeeding syllables, there is implied that emotion which contemplation of the object produces, and the emotion thus implied is, by sympathy, communicated. One may say that in the case of these two words, if the imposingness is alone to be considered, the word " magnificent " may with advantage be employed; but if the sentence expresses a proposition in which, not the imposingness itself, but something *about* the imposingness, is to be expressed, then the word " grand " is preferable.

The second qualification above referred to concerns the superiority of words derived from Latin or Greek, in cases where more or less abstract ideas have to be expressed. In such cases it is undesirable to use words having concrete associations; for such words, by the very vividness with which they call up thoughts of particular objects or particular actions, impede the formation of conceptions which refer, not to particular objects and actions, but to general truths concerning objects or actions of kinds that are more or less various. Thus, such an expression as " the colligation of facts " is better for philosophical purposes than such an expression as " the tying together of facts." This last expression cannot be used without suggesting the thought of a bundle of material things bound up by a string or cord—a thought which, in so far as the materiality of its components is concerned, conflicts with the conception to be suggested. Though it is true that, when its derivation is remembered, " colligation " raises the same thought, yet, as the thought is not so promptly or irresistibly raised, it stands less in the way of the abstract conception with which attention should be exclusively occupied.

THE ORIGIN AND FUNCTION OF MUSIC

[*First published in* Fraser's Magazine *for October* 1857.]

WHEN Carlo, standing chained to his kennel, sees his master in the distance, a slight motion of the tail indicates his but faint hope that he is about to be let out. A much more decided wagging of the tail, passing by-and-by into lateral undulations of the body, follows his master's nearer approach. When hands are laid on his collar and he knows that he is really to have an outing, his jumping and wriggling are such that it is by no means easy to loose his fastenings. And when he finds himself actually free, his joy expends itself in bounds, in pirouettes, and in scourings hither and thither at the top of his speed. Puss too, by erecting her tail, and by every time raising her back to meet the caressing hand of her mistress, similarly expresses her gratification by certain muscular actions; as likewise do the parrot by awkward dancings on his perch, and the canary by hopping and fluttering about his cage with unwonted rapidity. Under emotions of an opposite kind, animals equally display muscular excitement. The enraged lion lashes his sides with his tail, knits his brows, protrudes his claws. The cat sets up her back; the dog retracts his upper lip; the horse throws back his ears. And in the struggles of creatures in pain we see that a like relation holds between excitement of the muscles and excitement of the nerves of sensation.

In ourselves, distinguished from lower creatures by

feelings alike more powerful and more varied, parallel facts are at once more conspicuous and more numerous. Let us look at them in groups. We shall find that pleasurable sensations and painful sensations, pleasurable emotions and painful emotions, all tend to produce active demonstrations in proportion to their intensity.

In children, and even in adults who are not restrained by regard for appearances, a highly agreeable taste is followed by a smacking of the lips. An infant will laugh and bound in its nurse's arms at the sight of a brilliant colour or the hearing of a new sound. People are apt to beat time with head or feet to music which particularly pleases them. In a sensitive person an agreeable perfume will produce a smile; and smiles will be seen on the faces of a crowd gazing at some splendid burst of fireworks. Even the pleasant sensation of warmth felt on getting to the fireside out of a winter's storm will similarly express itself in the face.

Painful sensations, being mostly far more intense than pleasurable ones, cause muscular actions of much more decided kinds. A sudden twinge produces a convulsive start of the whole body. A pain less violent, but continuous, is accompanied by a knitting of the brows, a setting of the teeth, or biting of the lip, and a contraction of the features generally. Under a persistent pain of a severer kind other muscular actions are added: the body is swayed to and fro; the hands clench anything they can lay hold of; and should the agony rise still higher, the sufferer rolls about on the floor almost convulsed.

Though more varied, the natural language of the

pleasurable emotions comes within the same generalization. A smile, which is the commonest expression of gratified feeling, is a contraction of certain facial muscles; and when the smile broadens into a laugh we see a more violent and more general muscular excitement produced by an intenser gratification. Rubbing together of the hands, and that other motion which Hood describes as the washing of " hands with invisible soap in imperceptible water," have like implications. Children may often be seen to " jump for joy." Even in adults of excitable temperament an action approaching to it is sometimes witnessed. And dancing has all the world through been regarded as natural to an elevated state of minds. Many of the special emotions show themselves in special muscular actions. The gratification resulting from success raises the head and gives firmness to the gait. A hearty grasp of the hand is currently taken as indicative of friendship. Under a gush of affection the mother clasps her child to her breast, feeling as though she could squeeze it to death. And so in sundry other cases. Even in that brightening of the eye with which good news is received we may trace the same truth; for this sparkling appearance is due to an extra contraction of the muscle which raises the eyelid, and so allows more light to fall upon and be reflected from the wet surface of the eyeball.

The bodily indications of painful emotion are equally numerous and still more vehement. Discontent is shown by raised eyebrows and wrinkled forehead; disgust by a curl of the lip; offence by a pout. The impatient man beats a tattoo with his fingers on the table, swings his pendant leg with increasing rapidity, gives needless pokings to the fire, and presently paces with hasty strides about the room. In great grief there is wringing of the hands, and even tearing of the hair. An angry child stamps, or rolls on its back and kicks its heels in the air; and in manhood, anger, first showing itself in frowns, in distended nostrils, in compressed lips, goes on to produce grinding of the teeth, clenching of the fingers, blows of the fist on the table, and perhaps ends in a violent attack on the offending person, or in throwing about and breaking the furniture. From that pursing of the mouth indicative of slight displeasure, up to the frantic struggles of the maniac, we find that mental irritation tends to vent itself in bodily activity.

All feelings, then—sensations or emotions, pleasurable or painful—have this common characteristic that they are muscular stimuli. Not forgetting the few apparently exceptional cases in which emotions exceeding a certain intensity produce prostration, we may set it down as a general law that alike in man and animals there is a direct connexion between feeling and movement, the last growing more vehement as the first grows more intense. Were it allowable here to treat the matter scientifically, we might trace this general law to the principle known among physiologists as that of *reflex action*.[1] Without doing this, however, the above numerous instances justify the generalization that every kind of mental excitement ends in excitement of the muscles; and that the two preserve a more or less constant ratio to each other.

[1] Those who seek information on this point may find it in an interesting tract by Mr. Alexander Bain, on *Animal Instinct and Intelligence*.

" But what has all this to do with the *The Origin and Function of Music ?* " asks the reader.   Very much, as we shall presently see.   All music is originally vocal. All vocal sounds are produced by the agency of certain muscles.   These muscles, in common with those of the body at large, are excited to contraction by pleasurable and painful feelings.   And therefore it is that feelings demonstrate themselves in sounds as well as in movements.   Therefore it is that Carlo barks as well as leaps when he is let out; that puss purrs as well as erects her tail;   that the canary chirps as well as flutters.   Therefore it is that the angry lion roars while he lashes his sides, and the dog growls while he retracts his lip.   Therefore it is that the maimed animal not only struggles, but howls.   And it is from this cause that in human beings bodily suffering expresses itself not only in contortions, but in shrieks and groans;   that in anger and fear and grief the gesticulations are accompanied by shouts and screams; that delightful sensations are followed by exclamations; and that we hear screams of joy and shouts of exultation.

We have here, then, a principle underlying all vocal phenomena, including those of vocal music and by consequence those of music in general.   The muscles that move the chest, larynx, and vocal chords, contracting like other muscles in proportion to the intensity of the feelings;   every different contraction of these muscles involving, as it does, a different adjustment of the vocal organs;   every different adjustment of the vocal organs causing a change in the sound emitted; it follows that variations of voice are the physiological results of variations of feeling.   It follows that each inflection or modulation is the natural outcome of some passing emotion or sensation; and it follows that the explanation of all kinds of vocal expression must be sought in this general relation between mental and muscular excitements.   Let us, then, see whether we cannot thus account for the chief peculiarities in the utterance of the feelings; grouping these peculiarities under the heads of *loudness, quality or timbre, pitch, intervals*, and *rate of variation*.

Between the lungs and the organs of voice there is much the same relation as between the bellows of an organ and its pipes.   And as the loudness of the sound given out by an organ-pipe increases with the strength of the blast from the bellows, so, other things equal, the loudness of a vocal sound increases with the strength of the blast from the lungs.   But the expulsion of air from the lungs is effected by certain muscles of the chest and abdomen.   The force with which these muscles contract is proportionate to the intensity of the feeling experienced.   Hence, *a priori*, loud sounds will be the results of strong feelings.   That they are so we have daily proof.   The pain, which, if moderate, can be borne silently, causes outcries if it becomes extreme.   While a slight vexation makes a child whimper, a fit of passion calls forth a howl that disturbs the neighbourhood.   When the voices in an adjacent room become unusually audible, we infer anger or surprise or joy.   Loudness of applause is significant of great approbation, and with uproarious mirth we associate the idea of high enjoyment.   Commencing with the silence of apathy, we find that the utterances grow louder as the sensations or emotions, whether pleasurable or painful, grow stronger.

That different *qualities* of voice accompany different mental states, and that under states of excitement the tones are more sonorous than usual, is another general fact admitting of a parallel explanation. The sounds of common conversation have but little resonance; those of stromg feeling have much more. Under rising ill-temper the voice acquires a metallic ring. In accordance with her constant mood the ordinary speech of a virago has a piercing quality quite opposite to that softness indicative of placidity. A ringing laugh marks joyous temperament. Grief unburdening itself uses tones approaching in *timbre* to those of chanting, and in his most pathetic passages an eloquent speaker similarly falls into tones more vibratory than those common to him. Now any one may readily convince himself that resonant vocal sounds can be produced only by a certain muscular effort additional to that ordinarily needed. If after uttering a word in his speaking voice the reader, without changing the pitch or the loudness, will *sing* this word, he will perceive that before he can sing it he has to alter the adjustment of the vocal organs, to do which a certain force must be used; and by putting his fingers on that external prominence marking the top of the larynx, he will have further evidence that to produce a sonorous tone the organs must be drawn out of their usual position. Thus, then, the fact that the tones of excited feeling are more vibratory than those of common conversation is another instance of the connexion between mental excitement and muscular excitement. The speaking voice, the recitative voice, and the singing voice, severally exemplify one general principle.

That the *pitch* of the voice varies according to the

action of the vocal muscles scarcely needs saying. All know that the middle notes in which they converse are made without appreciable effort, and all know that to make either very high notes or very low notes requires considerable effort. In either ascending or descending from the pitch of ordinary speech we are conscious of increasing muscular strain, which at each extreme of the register becomes painful. Hence it follows from our general principle that, while indifference or calmness will use the medium tones, the tones used during excitement will be either above or below them, and will rise higher and higher, or fall lower and lower, as the feelings grow stronger. This physiological deduction we also find to be in harmony with familiar facts. The habitual sufferer utters his complaints in a voice raised considerably above the natural key, and agonizing pain vents itself in either shrieks or groans— in very high or very low notes. Beginning at his talking pitch, the cry of the disappointed urchin grows more shrill as it grows louder. The " Oh! " of astonishment or delight begins several notes below the middle voice and descends still lower. Anger expresses itself in high tones, or else in " curses not loud but *deep.*" Deep tones, too, are always used in uttering strong reproaches. Such an exclamation as " Beware! " if made dramatically—that is, if made with a show of feeling—must be many notes lower than ordinary. Further, we have groans of disapprobation, groans of horror, groans of remorse. And extreme joy and fear are alike accompanied by shrill outcries.

Nearly allied to the subject of pitch is that of *intervals,* and the explanation of them carries our argument a step further. While calm speech is comparatively monotonous, emotion makes use of fifths, octaves, and even wider intervals. Listen to any one narrating or repeating something in which he has no interest, and his voice will not wander more than two or three notes above or below his medium note, and that by small steps; but when he comes to some exciting event he will be heard not only to use the higher and lower notes of his register, but to go from one to the other by larger leaps. Being unable in print to imitate these traits of feeling, we feel some difficulty in fully conveying them to the reader. But we may suggest a few remembrances which will perhaps call to mind a sufficiency of others. If two men living in the same place, and frequently seeing one another, meet, say at a public assembly, any phrase with which one accosts the other—as " Hallo, are you here? "—will have an ordinary intonation. But if one of them, after a long absence, has unexpectedly returned, the expression of surprise with which his friend greets him —"Hallo! how came you here? "—will be uttered in much more strongly contrasted tones. The two syllables of the word " Hallo " will be, the one much higher, and the other much lower than before, and the rest of the sentence will similarly ascend and descend by longer steps. Again, if, supposing her maid to be in an adjoining room, the mistress of the house calls " Mary," the two syllables of the name will be spoken in an ascending interval of a third. If Mary does not reply, the call will be repeated probably in a descending fifth, implying the slightest shade of annoyance at Mary's inattention. Should Mary still make no answer, the increasing annoyance will show itself by the use of a descending octave on the next repetition of the call. And supposing the silence to continue, the lady, if not of a very even temper, will show her irritation at Mary's seemingly intentional negligence by finally calling her in tones still more widely contrasted —the first syllable being higher and the last lower than before. Now, these and analogous facts, which the reader will readily accumulate, clearly conform to the law laid down. For to make large intervals requires more muscular action than to make small ones. But not only is the *extent* of vocal intervals thus explicable as due to the relation between nervous and muscular excitement, but also in some degree their *direction*, as ascending or descending. The middle notes being those which demand no appreciable effort of muscular adjustment, and the effort becoming greater as we either ascend or descend, it follows that a departure from the middle notes in either direction will mark increasing emotion, while a return towards the middle notes will mark decreasing emotion. Hence it happens that an enthusiastic person, uttering such a sentence as " It was the most splendid sight I ever saw! " will ascend to the first syllable of the word " splendid," and thence will descend, the word " splendid " marking the climax of the feeling produced by the recollection. Hence, again, it happens that, under some extreme vexation produced by another's stupidity, an irascible man, exclaiming " What a confounded fool the fellow is! " will begin somewhat below his middle voice, and descending to the word " fool," which he will utter in one of his deepest notes, will then ascend. And it may be remarked that the word " fool " will not only be deeper and louder than the rest, but will also have more emphasis of articulation—another mode in which muscular excitement is shown. There is some danger, however, in giving instances like this; seeing that as the mode of rendering will vary according to the intensity of the feeling which the reader feigns to himself, the right cadence may not be hit upon. With single words there is less difficulty. Thus the " Indeed ! " with which a surprising fact is received mostly begins on the middle note of the voice, and rises with the second syllable; or, if disapprobation as well as astonishment is felt, the first syllable will be below the middle note and the second lower still. Conversely, the word " Alas ! " which marks not the rise of a paroxysm of grief but its decline, is uttered in a cadence descending towards the middle note; or, if the first syllable is in the lower part of the register, the second ascends towards the middle note. In the " Heigh-ho ! " expressive of mental or muscular prostration we may see the same truth; and if the cadence appropriate to it be inverted, the absurdity of the effect clearly shows how the meaning of intervals is dependent on the principle we have been illustrating.

The remaining characteristic of emotional speech which we have to notice is that of *variability of pitch.* It is scarcely possible here to convey adequate ideas of this more complex manifestation. We must be content with simply indicating some occasions on which it may be observed. On a meeting of friends, for instance—as when there arrives a party of much-wished-for visitors—the voices of all will be heard to undergo changes of pitch not only greater but much more numerous than usual. If a speaker at a public meeting is interrupted by some squabble among those he is addressing, his comparatively level tones will be

E

in marked contrast with the rapidly changing ones of the disputants. And among children, whose feelings are less under control than those of adults, this peculiarity is still more decided. During a scene of complaint and recrimination between two excitable little. girls, the voices may be heard to run up and down the gamut several times in each sentence. In such cases we once more recognize the same law: for muscular excitement is shown not only in strength of contraction, but also in the rapidity with which different muscular adjustments succeed one another.

Thus we find all the leading vocal phenomena to have a physiological basis. They are so many manifestations of the general law that feeling is a stimulus to muscular action—a law conformed to throughout the whole economy, not of man only, but of every sensitive creature—a law, therefore, which lies deep in the nature of animal organization. The expressiveness of these various modifications of voice is therefore innate. Each of us, from babyhood upwards, has been spontaneously making them when under the various sensations and emotions by which they are produced. Having been conscious of each feeling at the same time that we heard ourselves make the consequent sound, we have acquired an established association of ideas between such sound and the feeling which caused it. When the like sound is made by another, we ascribe the like feeling to him; and by a further consequence we not only ascribe to him that feeling, but have a certain degree of it aroused in ourselves; for to become conscious of the feeling which another is experiencing is to have that feeling awakened in our own consciousness, which is the same thing as experiencing the feeling. Thus these various modifications of voice become not only a language through which we understand the emotions of others, but also the means of exciting our sympathy with such emotions.

Have we not here, then, adequate data for a theory of music? These vocal peculiarities which indicate excited feeling *are those which especially distinguish song from ordinary speech.* Every one of the alterations of voice which we have found to be a physiological result of pain or pleasure *is carried to an extreme in vocal music.* For instance, we saw that, in virtue of the general relation between mental and muscular excitement, one characteristic of passionate utterance is *loudness.* Well, its comparative loudness is one of the distinctive marks of song as contrasted with the speech of daily life. Though there are *piano* passages in contrast with the *forte* passages, yet the average loudness of the singing voice is much greater than that of the speaking voice; and further, the *forte* passages of an air are those intended to represent the climax of its emotion. We next saw that the tones in which emotion expresses itself are, in conformity with this same law, of a more sonorous *timbre* than those of calm conversation. Here, too, song displays a still higher degree of the peculiarity; for the singing tone is the most resonant we can make. Again, it was shown that, from a like cause, mental excitement vents itself in the higher and lower notes of the register, using the middle notes but seldom. And it scarcely needs saying that vocal music is still more distinguished by its comparative neglect of the notes in which we talk and its habitual use of those above or below them;

and, moreover, that its most passionate effects are commonly produced at the two extremities of its scale, but especially at the upper one. A yet further trait of strong feeling, similarly accounted for, was the habitual employment of larger intervals than are employed in common converse. This trait, also, every ballad and *aria* systematically elaborates; add to which, that the direction of these intervals, which, as diverging from or converging towards the medium tones, we found to be physiologically expressive of increasing or decreasing emotion, may be observed to have in music like meanings. Once more it was pointed out that not only extreme but also rapid variations of pitch are characteristic of mental excitement; and once more we see, in the quick changes of every melody, that song carries the characteristic as far, if not farther. Thus, in respect alike of *loudness, timbre, pitch, intervals*, and *rate of variation*, song employs and exaggerates the natural language of the emotions; it arises from a systematic combination of those vocal pecularities which are the physiological effects of acute pleasure and pain.

Besides these chief characteristics of song as distinguished from common speech, there are sundry minor ones similarly applicable as due to the relation between mental and muscular excitement, and before proceeding further, these should be briefly noticed. Thus certain passions, and perhaps all passions when pushed to an extreme, produce (probably through their influence over the action of the heart) an effect the reverse of that which has been described: they cause a physical prostration, one symptom of which is a general relaxation of the muscles and a consequent trembling.

We have the trembling of anger, of fear, of hope, of joy; and the vocal muscles being implicated with the rest, the voice, too, becomes tremulous. Now, in singing, this tremulousness of voice is effectively used by some vocalists in pathetic passages; sometimes indeed, because of its effectiveness, too much used by them—as by Tamberlik, for instance. Again, there is a mode of musical execution known as the *staccato*, appropriate to energetic passages—to passages expressive of exhilaration, of resolution, of confidence. The action of the vocal muscles which produces this staccato style is analogous to the muscular action which produces the sharp, decisive, energetic movements of body indicating these states of mind; and therefore it is that the staccato style has the meaning we ascribe to it. Conversely, slurred intervals are expressive of gentler and less active feelings, and are so because they imply the smaller muscular vivacity due to a lower mental energy. The difference of effect resulting from difference of *time* in music is also attributable to this same law. Already it has been pointed out that the more frequent changes of pitch which ordinarily result from passion are imitated and developed in song; and here we have to add that the various rates of such changes appropriate to the different styles of music, are further traits having the same deviation. The slowest movements, *largo* and *adagio*, are used where such depressing emotions as grief, or such unexciting emotions as reverence, are to be portrayed; while the more rapid movements, *andante*, *allegro*, *presto*, represent successively increasing degrees of mental vivacity, and do this because they imply that muscular activity which flows from this mental vivacity. Even the *rhythm*, which forms a remaining distinction between song and speech, may not improbably have a kindred cause. Why the actions excited by strong feeling should tend to become rhythmical is not obvious, but that they do so there are divers evidences. There is the swaying of the body to and fro under pain or grief, of the leg under impatience or agitation. Dancing, too, is a rhythmical action natural to elevated emotion. That under excitement speech acquires a certain rhythm, we may occasionally perceive in the highest efforts of an orator. In poetry, which is a form of speech used for the better expression of emotional ideas, we have this rhythmical tendency developed. And when we bear in mind that dancing, poetry, and music are connate—are originally constituent parts of the same thing—it becomes clear that the measured movement common to them all implies a rhythmical action of the whole system, the vocal apparatus included; and that so the rhythm of music is a more subtle and complex result of this relation between mental and muscular excitement.

But it is time to end this analysis, which possibly we have already carried too far. It is not to be supposed that the more special peculiarities of musical expression are to be definitely explained. Though probably they may all in some way conform to the principle that has been worked out, it is impracticable to trace that principle in its more ramified applications. Nor is it needful to our argument that it should be so traced. The foregoing facts sufficiently prove that what we regard as the distinctive traits of song are simply the traits of emotional speech intensified and systematized. In respect of its general characteristics we think it has been made clear that vocal music, and by consequence all music, is an idealization of the natural language of passion.

As far as it goes, the scanty evidence furnished by history confirms this conclusion. Note first the fact (not properly an historical one, but fitly grouped with such) that the dance-chants of savage tribes are very monotonous; and in virtue of their monotony are more nearly allied to ordinary speech than are the songs of civilized races. Joining with this the fact that there are still extant, among boatmen and others in the East, ancient chants of a like monotonous character, we may infer that vocal music originally diverged from emotional speech in a gradual, unobtrusive manner; and this is the inference to which our argument points. From the characters of the intervals the same conclusion may be drawn.

The songs of savages in the lowest scale of civilization are generally confined to the compass of few notes, seldom extending beyond the interval of the *fifth*. Sometimes, however, a sudden transition into the octave occurs, especially in sudden exclamations, or where a word naturally dictates an emphatic raising of the voice. The *fifth* especially plays a prominent part in primitive vocal music. . . . But it must not be supposed that each interval is distinctly intoned: on the contrary, in the transition from one interval to another, all the intermediate intervals are slightly touched in a way somewhat similar to a violinist drawing his finger rapidly over the string from one note to another to connect them; and as the intervals themselves are seldom clearly defined, it will easily be understood how nearly impossible it is to write down such songs in our notation so as to convey a correct idea of their natural effect.[1]

Further evidence to the same effect is supplied by Greek history. The early poems of the Greeks—which, be it remembered, were sacred legends embodied in that rhythmical, metaphorical language which strong feeling excites—were not recited, but chanted: the tones and cadences were made musical by the same influences which made the speech poetical. By those who have investigated the matter this chanting is believed to have been not what we call singing, but nearly allied to our recitative—nearly allied but simpler. Several facts conspire to show this. The earliest stringed instruments had sometimes four, sometimes five strings: Egyptian frescoes delineate some of the simpler harps as thus constituted, and there are kindred representations of the lyres and allied instruments of the Assyrians, Hebrews, Greeks, and Romans. That the earliest Greek lyre had but four strings, and that the recitative of the poet was uttered in unison with its sounds, Neumann finds definite proof in a verse ascribed to Terpander, celebrating his introduction of the seven-stringed lyre:—

> The four-toned hymns now rejecting,
> And yearning for songs new and sweet,
> With seven strings softly vibrating,
> The lyre anon shall we greet.

Hence it follows that the primitive recitative was simpler than our modern recitative, and as such much

[1] *The Music of the Most Ancient Nations, etc.*, by Carl Engel. This quotation is not contained in my essay as originally published, nor in the version of it first reproduced in 1858. Herr Engel's work was issued in 1864, seven years after the date of the essay.

less remote from common speech than our own singing is. For recitative or musical recitation is in all
respects intermediate between speech and song. Its
average effects are not so *loud* as those of song. Its
tones are less sonorous in *timbre* than those of song.
Commonly it diverges to a smaller extent from the
middle notes—uses notes neither so high nor so low in
pitch. The *intervals* habitual to it are neither so wide
nor so varied. Its *rate of variation* is not so rapid.
And at the same time that its primary *rhythm* is less
decided, it has none of that secondary rhythm produced by recurrence of the same or parallel musical
phrases, which is one of the marked characteristics of
song. Thus, then, we may not only infer, from the
evidence furnished by existing barbarous tribes, that
the vocal music of pre-historic times was emotional
speech very slightly exalted; but we see that the earliest
vocal music of which we have any account, differed
much less from emotional speech than does the vocal
music of our days.

That recitative—beyond which, by the way, the
Chinese and Hindoos seem never to have advanced—
grew naturally out of the modulations and cadences
of strong feeling, we have indeed current evidence.
There are even now to be met with occasions on which
strong feeling vents itself in this form. Whoever has
been present when a meeting of Quakers was addressed
by one of their number (whose practice it is to speak
under the influence of religious emotion) must have
been struck by the quite unusual tones, like those of a
subdued chant, in which the address was made. On
passing a chapel in Wales during service, the raised and
sing-song voice of the preacher draws the attention.

It is clear, too, that the intoning used in churches is representative of this mental state, and has been adopted on account of the congruity between it and the contrition, supplication, or reverence verbally expressed.

And if, as we have good reason to believe, recitative arose by degrees out of emotional speech, it becomes manifest that by a continuance of the same process song has arisen out of recitative. Just as, from the orations and legends of savages, expressed in the metaphorical, allegorical style natural to them, there sprung epic poetry, out of which lyric poetry was afterwards developed; so, from the exalted tones and cadences in which such orations and legends were delivered, came the chant or recitative music, from which lyrical music has since grown up. And there has not only thus been a simultaneous and parallel genesis, but there has been reached a parallelism of results. For lyrical poetry differs from epic poetry, just as lyrical music differs from recitative: each still further intensifies the natural language of the emotions. Lyrical poetry is more metaphorical, more hyperbolic, more elliptical, and adds the rhythm of lines to the rhythm of feet; just as lyrical music is louder, more sonorous, more extreme in its intervals, and adds the rhythm of phrases to the rhythm of bars. And the known fact that out of epic poetry the stronger passions developed lyrical poetry as their appropriate vehicle, strengthens the inference that they similarly developed lyrical music out of recitative.

Nor indeed are we without evidences of the transition. It needs but to listen to an opera to hear the leading gradations. Between the comparatively level recitative of ordinary dialogue, the more varied recitative with wider intervals and higher tones used in exciting scenes, the still more musical recitative which preludes an air, and the air itself, the successive steps are but small; and the fact that among airs themselves gradations of like nature may be traced, further confirms the conclusion that the highest form of vocal music was arrived at by degrees.

We have some clue to the influences which have induced this development, and may roughly conceive the process of it. As the tones, intervals, and cadences of strong emotion were the elements out of which song was elaborated, so we may expect to find that still stronger emotion produced the elaboration, and we have evidence implying this. Musical composers are men of acute sensibilities. The *Life of Mozart* depicts him as one of intensely active affections and highly impressionable temperament. Various anecdotes represent Beethoven as very susceptible and very passionate. Mendelssohn is described by those who knew him as having been full of fine feeling. And the almost incredible sensitiveness of Chopin has been illustrated in the memoirs of George Sand. An unusually emotional nature being thus the general characteristic of musical composers, we have in it just the agency required for the development of recitative and song. Any cause of excitement will generate just those exaggerations which we have found to distinguish the lower vocal music from emotional speech, and the higher vocal music from the lower. Thus it becomes credible that the four-toned recitative of the early Greek poets (like all poets, nearly allied to composers in the comparative intensity of their feelings) was really nothing more than the slightly exaggerated emotional speech natural to them, which grew by frequent use into an organized form.   And we may infer that the accumulated agency of subsequent poet-musicians, inheriting and adding to the products of those who went before them, sufficed in the course of many centuries to develop this simple four-toned recitative into a vocal music having great complexity and range.

Not only may we so understand how more sonorous tones, greater extremes of pitch, and wider intervals were gradually introduced, but also how there arose a greater variety and complexity of musical expression. For this same passionate, enthusiastic temperament, which leads the musical composer to express the feelings possessed by others as well as himself in more marked cadences than they would use, also leads him to give musical utterance to feelings which they either do not experience or experience in but slight degrees.   And thus we may in some measure understand how it happens that music not only so strongly excites our more familiar feelings, but also produces feelings we never had before—arouses dormant sentiments of which we do not know the meaning; or as Richter says—tells us of things we have not seen and shall not see.

Indirect evidences of several kinds remain to be briefly pointed out.   One of them is the difficulty, not to say impossibility, of otherwise accounting for the expressiveness of music.   Whence comes it that special combinations of notes should have special effects upon our emotions—that one should give us a feeling of exhilaration, another of melancholy, another of affection, another of reverence? Is it that these special combinations have intrinsic meanings apart from the human constitution?—that a certain number of aërial waves per second, followed by a certain other number, in the nature of things signify grief, while in the reverse order they signify joy; and similarly with all other intervals, phrases, and cadences? Few will be so irrational as to think this. Is it, then, that the meanings of these special combinations are conventional only; that we learn their implications, as we do those of words, by observing how others understand them? This is an hypothesis not only devoid of evidence, but directly opposed to the experience of every one, and it is excluded by the fact that children, unconventionalized though they are, show great susceptibility to music. How, then, are musical effects to be explained? If the theory above set forth be accepted, the difficulty disappears. If music, taking for its raw material the various modifications of voice which are the physiological results of excited feeling, intensifies, combines, and complicates them; if it exaggerates the loudness, the resonance, the pitch, the intervals, and the variability, which, in virtue of an organic law, are the characteristics of passionate speech; if, by carrying out these further, more consistently, more unitedly, and more sustainedly, it produces an idealized language of emotion; then its power over us becomes comprehensible. But in the absence of this theory the expressiveness of music appears inexplicable.

Again, the preference we feel for certain qualities of sound presents a like difficulty, admitting only of a like solution. It is generally agreed that the tones of the human voice are more pleasing than any others. If music takes its rise from the modulations of the human voice under emotion, it is a natural consequence that the tones of that voice appeal to our feelings more than any others, and are considered more beautiful than any others. But deny that music has this origin, and the only alternative is the untenable one that the vibrations proceeding from a vocalist's throat are, objectively considered, of a higher order than those from a horn or a violin.

Once more, the question, How is the expressiveness of music to be otherwise accounted for? may be supplemented by the question, How is the genesis of music to be otherwise accounted for? That music is a product of civilization is manifest; for though some of the lowest savages have their dance-chants, these are of a kind scarcely to be dignified by the title musical: at most they supply but the vaguest rudiment of music properly so called. And if music has been by slow steps developed in the course of civilization, it must have been developed out of something. If, then, its origin is not that above alleged, what is its origin?

Thus we find that the negative evidence confirms the positive, and that taken together they furnish strong proof. We have seen that there is a physiological relation common to man and all animals between feeling and muscular action; that as vocal sounds are produced by muscular action, there is a consequent physiological relation between feeling and vocal sounds; that all the modifications of voice expressive of feeling are the direct results of this physiological relation; that music, adopting all these modifications, intensifies them more and more as it ascends to its higher and higher forms; that from the ancient epic poet chanting his verses, down to the modern musical composer, men of unusually strong feelings, prone to express them in extreme forms, have been naturally the agents of these successive intensifications; and that so there has little by little arisen a wide divergence between this idealized language of emotion and its natural language: to which direct evidence we have just added the indirect—that on no other tenable hypothesis can either the expressiveness of music or the genesis of music be explained.

And now, what is the *function* of music? Has music any effect beyond the immediate pleasure it produces? Analogy suggests that it has. The enjoyments of a good dinner do not end with themselves, but minister to bodily well-being. Though people do not marry with a view to maintain the race, yet the passions which impel them to marry secure its maintenance. Parental affection is a feeling which, while it conduces to parental happiness, ensures the nurture of off-spring. Men love to accumulate property, often without thought of the benefits it produces; but in pursuing the pleasure of acquisition they indirectly open the way to other pleasures. The wish for public approval impels all of us to do many things which we should otherwise not do—to undertake great labours, face great dangers, and habitually rule ourselves in ways that smooth social intercourse; so that in grati-fying our love of approbation we subserve divers ulterior purposes. And generally our nature is such that, in fulfilling each desire, we in some way facilitate fulfilment of the rest.   But the love of music seems to exist for its own sake.   The delights of melody and harmony do not obviously minister to the welfare either of the individual or of society.   May we not suspect, however, that this exception is apparent only?   Is it not a rational inquiry, What are the indirect benefits which accrue from music, in addition to the direct pleasure it gives?

But that it would take us too far out of our track, we should prelude this inquiry by illustrating at some length a certain general law of progress—the law that alike in occupations, sciences, arts, the divisions which had a common root, but by gradual divergence have become distinct and are now being separately developed, are not truly independent, but severally act and react on one another in their mutual advancement. Merely hinting thus much, however, by way of showing that there are many analogies to justify us, we go on to express the opinion that there exists a relationship of this kind between music and speech.

All speech is compounded of two elements: the words and the tones in which they are uttered—the signs of ideas and the signs of feelings.   While certain articulations express the thought, certain modulations express the more or less of pain or pleasure which the thought gives.   Using the word *cadence* in an unusually extended sense, as comprehending all variations of voice, we may say that *cadence is the commentary of the emotions upon the propositions of the intellect*. This duality of spoken language, though not formally recognized, is recognized in practice by every one; and every one knows that very often more weight attaches to the tones than to the words. Daily experience supplies cases in which the same sentence of disapproval will be understood as meaning little or meaning much, according to the vocal inflections which accompany it; and daily experience supplies still more striking cases in which words and tones are in direct contradiction—the first expressing consent, while the last express reluctance; and the last being believed rather than the first.

These two distinct but interwoven elements of speech have been undergoing a simultaneous development. We know that in the course of civilization words have been multiplied, new parts of speech have been introduced, sentences have grown more varied and complex; and we may fairly infer that during the same time new modifications of voice have come into use, fresh intervals have been adopted, and cadences have become more elaborate. For while on the one hand it is absurd to suppose that, along with the undeveloped verbal forms of barbarism, there existed developed vocal inflections; it is, on the other hand, necessary to suppose that, along with the higher and more numerous verbal forms needed to convey the multiplied and complicated ideas of civilized life, there have grown up those more involved changes of voice which express the feelings proper to such ideas. If intellectual language is a growth, so also, without doubt, is emotional language a growth.

Now the hypothesis which we have hinted above is, that beyond the direct pleasure which it gives, music has the indirect effect of developing this language of the emotions. Having its root, as we have endeavoured to show, in those tones, intervals, and cadences of

F

speech which express feeling, arising by the combination and intensifying of these, and coming finally to have an embodiment of its own, music has all along been reacting upon speech, and increasing its power of rendering emotion. The use in recitative and song of inflections more expressive than ordinary ones, must from the beginning have tended to develop the ordinary ones. The complex musical phrases by which composers have conveyed complex emotions may rationally be supposed to influence us in making those involved cadences of conversation by which we convey our subtler thoughts and feelings. If the cultivation of music has any effect on the mind, what more natural effect is there than this of developing our perception of the meanings of qualities and modulations of voice, and giving us a correspondingly increased power of using them? Just as chemistry, arising out of the processes of metallurgy and the industrial arts and gradually growing into an independent study, has now become an aid to all kinds of production; just as physiology, originating from medicine and once subordinate to it, but latterly pursued for its own sake, is in our day coming to be the science on which the progress of medicine depends; so music, having its root in emotional language and gradually evolved from it, has ever been reacting upon and further advancing it.

It will scarcely be expected that much direct evidence in support of this conclusion can be given. The facts are of a kind which it is difficult to measure, and of which we have no records. Some suggestive traits, however, are to be noted. May we not say, for instance, that the Italians, among whom modern music was earliest cultivated, and who have more especially excelled in melody (the division of music with which our argument is chiefly concerned)—may we not say that these Italians speak in more varied and expressive inflections and cadences than any other people? On the other hand, may we not say that, confined almost exclusively as they have hitherto been to their national airs, and therefore accustomed to but a limited range of musical expression, the Scotch are unusually monotonous in the intervals and modulations of their speech? And again, do we not find, among different classes of the same nation, differences that have like implications? The gentleman and the clown stand in decided contrast with respect to variety of intonation. Listen to the conversation of a servant-girl and then to that of a refined lady, and the more delicate and complex changes of voice used by the latter will be conspicuous. Now without going so far as to say that out of all the differences of culture to which the upper and lower classes are subjected, difference of musical culture is that to which alone this difference of speech is ascribable; yet we may fairly say that there seems a much more obvious connexion of cause and effect between these than between any others. Thus, while the inductive evidence to which we can appeal is but scanty and vague, yet what there is favours our position.

Probably most will think that the function here assigned to music is one of very little moment. But reflection may lead them to a contrary conviction. In its bearings upon human happiness, this emotional language which musical culture develops and refines

is only second in importance to the language of the
intellect; perhaps not even second to it. For these
modifications of voice produced by feelings are the
means of exciting like feelings in others. Joined with
gestures and expressions of face, they give life to the
otherwise dead words in which the intellect utters its
ideas, and so enable the hearer not only to *understand*
the state of mind they accompany, but to *partake* of
that state. In short they are the chief media of *sympathy*. And if we consider how much both our general
welfare and our immediate pleasures depend on
sympathy, we shall recognize the importance of whatever makes this sympathy greater. If we bear in
mind that by their fellow-feeling men are led to behave
justly and kindly to one another; that the difference
between the cruelty of the barbarous and the humanity
of the civilized results from the increase of fellow-
feeling; if we bear in mind that this faculty which
makes us sharers in the joys and sorrows of others is the
basis of all the higher affections; if we bear in mind
how much our direct gratifications are intensified by
sympathy—how at the theatre, the concert, the picture
gallery, we lose half our enjoyment if we have no one
to enjoy with us; we shall see that the agencies which
communicate it can scarcely be overrated in value.
The tendency of civilization is to repress the antago-
nistic elements of our characters and to develop the
social ones; to curb our purely selfish desires and
exercise our unselfish ones; to replace private
gratifications by gratifications resulting from or involving the pleasures of others. And while by this
adaptation to the social state the sympathetic side of
our nature is being unfolded, there is simultaneously

growing up a language of sympathetic intercourse—a language through which we communicate to others the happiness we feel, and are made sharers in their happiness. This double process, of which the effects are already appreciable, must go on to an extent of which we can as yet have no adequate conception. The habitual concealment of our feelings diminishing, as it must, in proportion as our feelings become such as do not demand concealment, the exhibition of them will become more vivid than we now dare allow it to be; and this implies a more expressive emotional language. At the same time, feelings of higher and more complex kinds, as yet experienced only by the cultivated few, will become general, and there will be a corresponding development of the emotional language into more involved forms. Just as there has silently grown up a language of ideas which, rude as it at first was, now enables us to convey with precision the most subtle and complicated thoughts; so there is still silently growing up a language of feelings which, notwithstanding its present imperfection, we may expect will ultimately enable men vividly and completely to impress on each other the emotions which they experience from moment to moment.

Thus if, as we have endeavoured to show, it is the function of music to facilitate the development of this emotional language, we may regard music as an aid to the achievement of that higher happiness which it indistinctly shadows forth. Those vague feelings of unexperienced felicity which music arouses—those indefinite impressions of an unknown ideal life which it calls up—may be considered as a prophecy, the fulfilment of which music itself aids. The strange capacity which we have for being affected by melody and harmony may be taken to imply both that it is within the possibilities of our nature to realize those intenser delights they dimly suggest, and that they are in some way concerned in the realization of them. If so, the power and the meaning of music become comprehensible, but otherwise they are a mystery.

We will only add that if the probability of these corollaries be admitted, then music must take rank as the highest of the fine arts—as the one which, more than any other, ministers to human welfare. And thus, even leaving out of view the immediate gratifications it is hourly giving, we cannot too much applaud that musical culture which is becoming one of the characteristics of our age.

POSTSCRIPT.—An opponent, or partial opponent, of high authority, whose views were published some fourteen years after the above essay, must here be answered: I mean Mr. Darwin. Diligent and careful as an observer beyond naturalists in general, and still more beyond those who are untrained in research, his judgment on a question which must be decided by induction is one to be received with great respect. I think, however, examination will show that in this instance Mr. Darwin's observations are inadequate, and his reasonings upon them inconclusive. Swayed by his doctrine of sexual selection, he has leaned towards the view that music had its origin in the expression of amatory feeling, and has been led to over-estimate such evidence as he thinks favours that view, while ignoring the difficulties in its way and the large amount of evidence supporting another view. Before considering the special reasons for dissenting from his hypothesis, let us look at the most general reasons.

The interpretation of music which Mr. Darwin gives agrees with my own in supposing music to be developed from vocal noises, but differs in supposing a particular class of vocal noises to have originated it—the amatory class. I have aimed to show that music has its germs in the sounds which the voice emits under excitement, and eventually gains this or that character according to the kind of excitement; whereas Mr. Darwin argues that music arises from those sounds which the male makes during the excitements of courtship, that they are consciously made to charm the female, and that from the resulting combinations of sounds arise not love-music only but music in general. That certain tones of voice and cadences having some likeness of nature are spontaneously used to express grief, others to express joy, others to express affection, and others to express triumph or martial ardour, is undeniable. According to the view I have set forth, the whole body of these vocal manifestations of emotion form the root of music. According to Mr. Darwin's view, the sounds which are prompted by the amatory feeling only having originated musical utterance, there are derived from these all the other varieties of musical utterance which aim to express other kinds of feeling. This roundabout derivation has, I think, less probability than the direct derivation.

This antithesis and its implications will perhaps be more clearly understood on looking at the facts under their nervo-muscular aspect. Mr. Darwin recognizes the truth of the doctrine with which the foregoing essay sets out, that feeling discharges itself in action, saying of the air-breathing vertebrata that:—

> When the primeval members of this class were strongly excited and their muscles violently contracted, purposeless sounds would almost certainly have been produced; and these, if they proved in any way serviceable, might readily have been modified or intensified by the preservation of properly adapted variations. (*The Descent of Man*, vol. ii., p. 331.)

But though this passage recognizes the general relation between feelings and those muscular contractions which cause sounds, it does so inadequately; since it ignores on the one hand those loudest sounds which accompany intense sensations—the shrieks and groans of bodily agony; while on the other hand it ignores those multitudinous sounds not produced " under the excitement of love, rage, and jealousy," but which accompany ordinary amounts of feelings, various in their kinds. And it is because he does not bear in mind how a large proportion of vocal noises are caused by other excitements that Mr. Darwin thinks " a strong case can be made out that the vocal organs were primarily used and perfected in relation to the propagation of the species " (p. 330).

Certainly the animals around us yield but few facts countenancing his view. The cooing of pigeons may indeed be named in its support; and it may be contended that caterwauling furnishes evidence; though I doubt whether the sounds are made by the male to charm the female. But the howling of dogs has no relation to sexual excitements; nor has their barking, which is used to express emotion of almost any kind.

Pigs grunt sometimes through pleasurable expectation, sometimes during the gratifications of eating, sometimes from a general content while seeking about for food. The bleatings of sheep, again, occur under the promptings of various feelings, usually of no great intensity—social and maternal rather than sexual. The like holds with the lowing of cattle. Nor is it otherwise with poultry. The quacking of ducks indicates general satisfaction, and the screams occasionally vented by a flock of geese seem rather to express a wave of social excitement than anything else. Save after laying an egg, when the sounds have the character of triumph, the cluckings of a hen show content; and on various occasions cock-crowing apparently implies good spirits only. In all cases an overflow of nervous energy has to find vent; and while in some cases it leads to wagging of the tail, in others it leads to contraction of the vocal muscles. That this relation holds not of one kind of feeling but of many kinds, is a truth which seems to me at variance with the view " that the vocal organs were primarily used and perfected in relation to the propagation of the species."

The hypothesis that music had its origin in the amatory sounds made by the male to charm the female has the support of the popular idea that the singing of birds constitutes a kind of courtship—an idea adopted by Mr. Darwin when he says that " the male pours forth his full volume of song, in rivalry with other males, for the sake of captivating the female." Usually Mr. Darwin does not accept without criticism and verification the beliefs he finds current, but in this case he seems to have done so. Even cursory observation suffices to dissipate this belief—initiated, I suppose, by poets. In preparation for dealing with the matter I have made memoranda concerning various song-birds dating back to 1883. On February 7 of that year I heard a lark singing several times; and still more remarkably, during the mild winter of 1884 I saw one soar, and heard it sing, on January 10. Yet the lark does not pair till March. Having heard the red-breast near the close of August 1888, I noted the continuance of its song all through the autumn and winter up to Christmas eve, Christmas day, December 29, and again on January 18, 1889. How common is the singing of the thrush during mild weather in winter, everyone must have observed. The presence of thrushes behind my house has led to the making of notes on this point. The male sang in November 1889; I noted the song again on Christmas eve, again on January 13, 1890, and from time to time all through the rest of that month. I heard little of his song in February, which is the pairing season; and none at all, save a few notes early in the morning, during the period of rearing the young. But now that, in the middle of May, the young, reared in a nest in my garden, have sometime since flown, he has recommenced singing vociferously at intervals throughout the day; and doubtless, in conformity with what I have observed elsewhere, will go on singing till July. How marked is the direct relation between singing and the conditions which cause high spirits, is perhaps best shown by a fact I noted on December 4, 1888, when, the day being not only mild but bright, the copses on Holmwood Common, Dorking, were vocal just as on a spring day, with a chorus of birds of various kinds — robins, thrushes, chaffinches, linnets, and sundry others of which I did not know the names.   Ornithological works furnish verifying statements.   Wood states that the hedge-sparrow continues " to sing throughout a large portion of the year, and only ceasing during the time of the ordinary moult."   The song of the black-cap, he says, " is hardly suspended throughout the year; " and of caged birds which sing continuously, save when moulting, he names the grosbeak, the linnet, the goldfinch, and the siskin.

I think these facts show that the popular idea adopted by Mr. Darwin is untenable.   What, then, is the true interpretation?   Simply that, like the whistling and humming of tunes by boys and men, the singing of birds results from overflow of energy—an overflow which in both cases ceases under depressing conditions.   The relation between courtship and singing, so far as it can be shown to hold, is not a relation of cause and effect, but a relation of concomitance: the two are simultaneous results of the same cause.   Throughout the animal kingdom at large the commencement of reproduction is associated with an excess of those absorbed materials needful for self-maintenance, and with a consequent ability to devote a part to the maintenance of the species.   This constitutional state is one with which there goes a tendency to superfluous expenditure in various forms of action—unusual vivacity of every kind, including vocal vivacity. While we thus see why pairing and singing come to be associated, we also see why there is singing at other times when the feeding and weather are favourable; and why in some cases, as in those of the thrush and the robin, there is more singing after the breeding season than before or during the breeding season.

We are shown, too, why these birds, and especially the thrush, so often sing in the winter: the supply of worms on lawns and in gardens being habitually utilized by both, and thrushes having the further advantage that they are strong enough to break the shells of the hybernating snails—this last ability being connected with the fact that thrushes and blackbirds are the first among the singing birds to build. It remains only to add that the alleged singing of males against one another with the view of charming the females is open to parallel criticisms. How far this competition happens during the pairing season I have not observed, but it certainly happens out of the pairing season. I have several times heard blackbirds singing alternately in June. But the most conspicuous instance is supplied by the redbreasts. These habitually sing against one another during the autumn months, reply and rejoinder being commonly continued for five minutes at a time.

Even did the evidence support the popular view, adopted by Mr. Darwin, that the singing of birds is a kind of courtship—even were there good proof, instead of much disproof, that a bird's song is a developed form of the sexual sounds made by the male to charm the female—the conclusion would, I think, do little towards justifying the belief that human music has had a kindred origin. For, in the first place, the bird-type in general, developed as it is out of the reptilian type, is very remotely related to that type of the *Vertebrata* which ascends to Man as its highest exemplar; and, in the second place, song-birds belong, with but few exceptions, to the single order of *Insessores*—one order only of the many orders constituting the class. So that if the *Vertebrata* at large be represented by a tree of

which Man is the topmost twig, then it is at a considerable distance down the trunk that there diverges
the branch from which the bird-type is derived; and
the group of singing-birds forms but a terminal sub-
division of this branch—lies far out of the ascending
line which ends in Man. To give appreciable support to Mr. Darwin's view, we ought to find vocal
manifestations of the amatory feeling becoming more
pronounced as we ascend along that particular line of
inferior *Vertebrata* out of which Man has arisen.   Just
as we find other traits which pre-figure human traits
(instance arms and hands adapted for grasping) becoming more marked as we approach Man, so should
we find becoming more marked this sexual use of the
voice, which is supposed to end in human song.   But
we do not find this. The South-American monkeys
(" the Howlers," as they are sometimes called), which
in chorus make the woods resound for hours together
with their " dreadful concert," appear, according to
Rengger, to be prompted by no other desire than that
of making a noise. Mr. Darwin admits, too, that
this is generally the case with the gibbons: the only
exception he is inclined to make being in the case of
Hylobates agilis, which, on the testimony of Mr.
Waterhouse, he says ascends and descends the scale by
half-tones.[1] This comparatively musical set of sounds,

---

[1] It is far more probable that the ascents and descents made
by this gibbon consisted of indefinitely slurred tones.   To suppose that each was a series of definite semi-tones strains belief
to breaking-point; considering that among human beings the
great majority, even of those who have good ears, are unable
to go up or down the chromatic scale without being taught to
do so.   The achievement is one requiring considerable practice;
and that such an achievement should be spontaneous on the
part of a monkey is incredible.

he thinks, may be used to charm the female, though there is no evidence forthcoming that this is the case. When we remember that in the forms nearest to the human—the chimpanzees and the gorilla—there is nothing which approaches even thus far towards musical utterance, we see that the hypothesis has next to none of that support which ought to be forthcoming. Indeed in his *Descent of Man*, vol. ii., p. 332, Mr. Darwin himself says: " It is a surprising fact that we have not as yet any good evidence that these organs are used by male mammals to charm the females "—an admission which amounts to something like a surrender.

Even more marked is the absence of proof when we come to the human race itself—or rather, not absence of proof but presence of disproof. Here, from the *Descriptive Sociology*, where the authorities will be found under the respective heads, I quote a number of testimonies of travellers concerning primitive music, commencing with those referring to the lowest races.

" The songs of the natives [of Australia] . . . are chiefly made on the spur of the moment, and refer to something that has struck the attention at the time." " The Watchandies, seeing me much interested in the genus Eucalyptus, soon composed a song on this subject." The Fuegians are fond of music and generally sing in their boats, doubtless keeping time, as many primitive peoples do. " The principal subject of the songs of the Araucanians is the exploits of their heroes: " when at work their " song was simple, referring mostly to their labour," and was the same " for every occasion, whether the burden of the song be joy or sorrow." The Greenlanders sing of "their exploits in the chase" and "chant the deeds of their ancestors." "The Indians of the Upper Mississippi vocalize an incident, as ' They have brought us a fat dog' " ; then the chorus goes on for a minute. Of other North-American Indians we read : " the air which the women sang was pleasing . . . the men first gave out the words, which formed a consummate glorification of themselves." Among the Carriers (of North America) there are professed composers, who " turn their talent to good account on the occasion of a feast, when new airs are in great request." Of the New Zealanders we read: " The singing of such compositions [laments] resembles cathedral chanting." " Passing events are described by extemporaneous songs, which are preserved when good." " When men worked together appropriate airs were sung." When presenting a meal to travellers women would chant, " What shall be our food ? Shell-fish and fern-root, that is the root of the earth." Among the Sandwich Islanders " most of the traditions of remarkable events in their history are preserved in songs." When taught reading they could not " recite a lesson without chanting or singing it." Cook found the Tahitians had itinerant musicians who gave narrative chants quite unpremeditated. " A Samoan can hardly put his paddle in the water without striking up some chant." A chief of the Kyans, " Tamawan, jumped up, and, while standing, burst out into an extempore song, in which Sir James Brooke and myself, and last but not least the wonderful steamer, were mentioned with warm eulogies." In East Africa " the fisherman will accompany his paddle, the porter his trudge, and the housewife her task of rubbing down grain, with song." In singing, the East African " contents himself with improvising a few words without sense or rhyme and repeats them till they nauseate." Among the Dahomans any incident " from the arrival of a stranger to an earthquake " is turned into a song. When rowing, the Coast-negroes sing " either a description of some love intrigue or the praise of some woman celebrated for her beauty." In Loango " the women, as they till the field, make it echo with their rustic songs." Park says of the Bambarran: " they lightened their labours by songs, one of which was composed extempore; for I was myself the subject of it." " In some parts of Africa nothing is done except to the sound of music." " They are very expert in adapting the subjects of these songs to current events." The Malays "amuse all their leisure hours . . . with the repetition of songs, which are for the most part proverbs illustrated. . . . Some that they rehearse in a kind of recitative at their *bimbangs* or feasts are historical love-tales." A Sumatran maiden will sometimes begin a tender song and be answered by one of the young men. The ballads of the Kamtschadales are " inspired apparently by grief, love, or domestic feeling "; and their music conveys " a sensation of sorrow and vague, unavailing regret." Of their love-songs it is said " the women generally compose them." A Kirghiz " singer sits on one knee and sings in an unnatural tone of voice, his lay being usually of an amorous character." Of the Yakuts we are told " their style of singing is monotonous . . . their songs described the beauty of the landscape in terms which appeared to me exaggerated."

In these statements, which, omitting repetitions, are all which the *Descriptive Sociology* contains relevant to the issue, several striking facts are manifest. Among the lowest races the only musical utterances named are those which refer to the incidents of the moment, and seem prompted by feelings which those incidents produce. The derivation of song or chant from emotional speech in general, thus suggested, is similarly suggested by the habits of many higher races; for they, too, show us that the musically-expressed feelings relevant to the immediate occasion, or to past occasions, are feelings of various kinds: now of simple good spirits and now of joy or triumph—now of surprise, praise, admiration, and now of sorrow, melancholy, regret. Only among certain of the more advanced races, as the semi-civilized Malays and peoples of Northern Asia, do we read of love-songs; and then, strange to say, these are mentioned as mostly coming not from men but from women. Out of all the testimonies there is not one which tells of a love-song spontaneously commenced by a man to charm a woman. Entirely absent among the rudest types and many of the more developed types, amatory musical utterance, where first found, is found under a form opposite to that which Mr. Darwin's hypothesis implies; and we have to seek among civilized peoples before we meet, in serenades and the like, music of the kind which, according to his view, should be the earliest.[1]

[1] After the above paragraphs had been sent to the printers I received from an American anthropologist, the Rev. Owen Dorsey, some essays containing kindred evidence. Of over three dozen songs and chants of the Omaha, Ponka, and other Indians, in some cases given with music and in other cases

G

Even were his view countenanced by the facts, there would remain unexplained the process by which sexually-excited sounds have been evolved into music. In the foregoing essay I have indicated the various qualities, relations, and combinations of tones, spontaneously prompted by emotions of all kinds, which exhibit in undeveloped forms the traits of recitative and melody. To have reduced his hypothesis to a shape admitting of comparison, Mr. Darwin should have shown that the sounds excited by sexual emotions possess these same traits; and, to have proved that his hypothesis is the more tenable, should have shown that they possess these same traits in a greater degree. But he has not attempted to do this. He has simply suggested that instead of having its roots in the vocal sounds caused by feelings of all kinds, music has its roots in the vocal sounds caused by the amatory feeling only; giving no reason why the effects of the feelings at large should be ignored, and the effects of one particular feeling alone recognized.

Nineteen years after my essay on *The Origin and Function of Music* was published, Mr. Edmund Gurney criticized it in an article which made its appearance in the *Fortnightly Review* for July 1876. Absorption in more important work prevented me from replying. Though some ten years ago I thought of defending my views against those of Mr. Darwin and Mr. Gurney, the occurrence of Mr. Darwin's death obliged

---

without, there are but five which have any reference to amatory feeling; and while in these the expression of amatory feeling comes from women, nothing more than derision of them comes from men.

me to postpone for a time any discussion of his views; and then the more recent unfortunate death of Mr. Gurney caused a further postponement. I must now, however, say that which seems needful, though there is no longer any possibility of a rejoinder from him.

Some parts of Mr. Gurney's criticism I have already answered by implication; for he adopts the hypothesis that music originated in the vocal utterances prompted by sexual feeling. To the reasons above given for rejecting this hypothesis I will add here what I might have added above, that it is at variance with one of the fundamental laws of evolution. All development proceeds from the general to the special. First there appear those traits which a thing has in common with many other things; then those traits which it has in common with a smaller class of things; and so on until there eventually arise those traits which distinguish it from everything else. The genesis which I have described conforms to this fundamental law. It posits the antecedent fact that feeling in general produces muscular contraction in general; and the less general fact that feeling in general produces, among other muscular contractions, those which move the respiratory and vocal apparatus. With these it joins the still less general fact that sounds indicative of feelings vary in sundry respects according to the intensity of the feelings, and then enumerates the still less general facts which show us the kinship between the vocal manifestations of feeling and the characters of vocal music—the implication being that there has gone on a progressive specialization. But the view which Mr. Gurney adopts from Mr. Darwin is that from the special actions producing the special sounds accompanying sexual excitement were evolved those various actions producing the various sounds which accompany all other feelings. Vocal expression of a particular emotion came first, and from this proceeded vocal expressions of emotions in general—the order of evolution was reversed.

To deficient knowledge of the laws of evolution are due sundry of Mr. Gurney's objections. He makes a cardinal error in assuming that a more evolved thing is distinguished from less evolved things in respect of *all* the various traits of evolution; whereas, very generally, a higher degree of evolution in some or most respects is accompanied by an equal or lower degree of evolution in other respects. On the average, increase of locomotive power goes along with advance of evolution; and yet numerous mammals are more fleet than man. The stage of development is largely indicated by degree of intelligence; and yet the more intelligent parrot is inferior in vision, in speed, and in destructive appliances, to the less-intelligent hawk. The contrast between birds and mammals well illustrates the general truth. A bird's skeleton diverges more widely from the skeleton of the lower vertebrates in respect of heterogeneity than does the skeleton of a mammal; and the bird has a more developed respiratory system, as well as a higher temperature of blood, and a superior power of locomotion. Nevertheless many mammals, in respect of bulk, in respect of various appliances (especially for prehension), and in respect of intelligence, are more evolved than birds. Thus it is obviously a mistake to assume that whatever is more highly evolved in general character is more highly evolved in every trait.

Of Mr. Gurney's several objections which are based on this mistake here is an example. He says: " Loudness though a frequent is by no means a universal or essential element, either of song or of emotional speech " (p. 107). Under one of its aspects this criticism is self-destructive; for if, though both relatively loud in most cases, song and emotional speech are both characterized by the occasional use of subdued tones, then this is a further point of kinship between them—a kinship which Mr. Gurney seeks to disprove. Under its other aspect this criticism implies the above-described misconception. If in a song, or rather in some part or parts of a song, the trait of loudness is absent, while the other traits of developed emotional utterances are present, it simply illustrates the truth that the traits of a highly evolved product are frequently not all present together.

A like answer is at hand to the next objection he makes. It came thus:—

> In the recitative which he [Mr. Spencer] himself onsiders naturally and historically a step between speech and song, the rapid variation of pitch is impossible, and such recitative is distinguished from the tones even of common speech precisely by being more monotonous (p. 108).

But Mr. Gurney overlooks the fact that while, in recitative, some traits of developed emotional utterance are not present, two of its traits are present. One is that greater resonance of tone, caused by greater contraction of the vocal chords, which distinguishes it from ordinary speech. The other is the relative elevation of pitch, or divergence from the medium tones of voice—a trait similarly implying greater strain of certain vocal muscles, resulting from stronger feeling.

Another difficulty raised by Mr. Gurney he would probably not have set down had he been aware that one character of musical utterance which he thinks distinctive is a character of all phenomena into which motion enters as a factor. He says: " Now no one can suppose that the sense of rhythm can be derived from emotional speech " (p. 110). Had he referred to the chapter on " The Rhythm of Motion," in *First Principles*, he would have seen that, in common with inorganic actions, all organic actions are completely or partially rhythmical—from appetite and sleep to inspirations and heart-beats; from the winking of the eyes to the contractions of the intestines; from the motions of the legs to discharges through the nerves. Having contemplated such facts, he would have seen that the rhythmical tendency which is perfectly displayed in musical utterance is imperfectly displayed in emotional speech. Just as under emotion we see swayings of the body and wringings of the hands, so do we see contractions of the vocal organs which are now stronger and now weaker. Surely it is manifest that the utterances of passion, far from being monotonous, are characterized by rapidly recurring ascents and descents of tone and by rapidly recurring emphases— there is rhythm, though it is an irregular rhythm.

Want of knowledge of the principles of evolution has, in another place, led Mr. Gurney to represent as an objection what is in reality a verification. He says:—

> Music is distinguished from emotional speech in that it proceeds not only by fixed degrees in time, but by fixed degrees in the scale. This is a con-

stant quality through all the immense quantity of embryo and developed scale-systems that have been used; whereas the transitions of pitch which mark emotional affections of voice are as Helmholtz has pointed out of a gliding character (p. 113).

Had Mr. Gurney known that evolution in all cases is from the indefinite to the definite, he would have seen that as a matter of course the gradations of emotional speech must be indefinite in comparison with the gradations of developed music. Progress from the one to the other is in part *constituted* by increasing definiteness in the time-intervals and increasing definiteness in the tone-intervals. Were it otherwise the hypothesis I have set forth would lack one of its evidences. To his allegation that not only the " developed scale-systems " but also the " embryo " scale-systems are definite, it may obviously be replied that the mere existence of any scale-system capable of being written down implies that the earlier stage of the progress has already been passed through. To have risen to a scale-system is to have become definite; and until a scale-system has been reached vocal phrases cannot have been recorded. Moreover had Mr. Gurney remembered that there are many people with musical perceptions so imperfect that when making their merely recognizable, and sometimes hardly recognizable, attempts to whistle or hum melodies, they show how vague are their appreciations of musical intervals, he would have seen reason for doubting his assumption that definite scales were reached all at once. The fact that in what we call bad ears there are all degrees of imperfection, joined with the fact that, where the imperfection is not great, practice may remedy it, suffice of themselves to show that definite perceptions of musical intervals were reached by degrees.

Some of Mr. Gurney's objections are strangely insubstantial. Here is an example:—

> The fact is that song, which moreover in our time is but a limited branch of music, is perpetually making conscious efforts; for instance, the most peaceful melody may be a considerable strain to a soprano voice, if sung in a very high register: while speech continues to obey in a natural way the physiological laws of emotion (p. 117).

That in exaggerating and emphasizing the traits of emotional speech the singer should be led to make " conscious efforts " is surely natural enough. What would Mr. Gurney have said of dancing? He would scarcely have denied that saltatory movements often result spontaneously from excited feeling; and he could hardly have doubted that primitive dancing arose as a systematized form of such movements. Would he have considered the belief that stage-dancing is evolved from these spontaneous movements to be negatived by the fact that a stage-dancer's bounds and gyrations are made with " conscious efforts " ?

In his elaborate work on *The Power of Sound*, Mr. Gurney, repeating in other forms the objections I have above dealt with, adds to them some others. One of these, which appears at first sight to have much weight, I must not pass by. He thus expresses it:—

> Any one may convince himself that not only are the intervals used in emotional speech very

large, twelve diatonic notes being quite an ordinary skip, but that he uses extremes of both high and low pitch with his speaking voice, which, if he tries to dwell on them and make them resonant, will be found to lie beyond the compass of his singing voice (p. 470).

Now the part of my hypothesis which Mr. Gurney here combats is that, as in emotional speech, so in song, feeling, by causing muscular contractions, causes divergencies from the middle tones of the voice, which become wider as it increases; and that this fact supports the belief that song is developed from emotional speech.   To this Mr. Gurney thinks it a conclusive answer that higher notes are used by the speaking voice than by the singing voice.   But if, as his words imply, there is a physical impediment to the production of notes in the one voice as high as those in the other, then my argument is justified if, in either voice, extremes of feeling are shown by extremes of pitch.   If, for example, the celebrated *ut de poitrine* with which Tamberlik brought down the house in one of the scenes of William Tell was recognized as expressing the greatest intensity of martial patriotism, my position is warranted even though in his speaking voice he could have produced a still higher note.

Of answers to Mr. Gurney's objections the two most effective are suggested by the passage in which he sums up his conclusions.   Here are his words:—

It is enough to recall how every consideration tended to the same result; that the oak grew from the acorn; that the musical faculty and pleasure, which have to do with music and nothing else, are the representatives and linear descendants of a faculty and pleasure which were musical and nothing else; and that, however rudely and tentatively applied to speech, Music was a *separate order* (p. 492).

Thus, then, it is implied that the true germs of music stand towards developed music as the acorn to the oak. Now suppose we ask, How many traits of the oak are to be found in the acorn? Next to none. And then suppose we ask, How many traits of music are to be found in the tones of emotional speech? Very many. Yet while Mr. Gurney thinks that music had its origin in something which might have been as unlike it as the acorn is unlike the oak, he rejects the theory that it had its origin in something as much like it as the cadences of emotional speech; and he does this because there are sundry differences between the characters of speech-cadences and the characters of music. In the one case he tacitly assumes a great unlikeness between germ and product; while in the other case he objects because germ and product are not in all respects similar!

I may end by pointing out how extremely improbable, *a priori*, is Mr. Gurney's conception. He admits, as perforce he must, that emotional speech has various traits in common with recitative and song—relatively greater resonance, relatively greater loudness, more marked divergences from medium tones, the use of the extremes of pitch in signifying the extremes of feeling, and so on. But, denying that the one is derived from the others, he implies that these kindred groups of traits have had independent origins. Two sets of peculiarities in the use of the voice which show various kinships, have nothing to do with one another! I think it merely requires to put the proposition in this shape to see how incredible it is.

Sundry objections to the views contained in the essay on *The Origin and Function of Music* have arisen from misconception of its scope. An endeavour to explain the *origin* of music has been dealt with as though it were a theory of music in its entirety. An hypothesis concerning the rudiments has been rejected because it did not account for everything contained in the developed product. To preclude this misapprehension for the future, and to show how much more is comprehended in a theory of music than I professed to deal with, let me enumerate the several components of musical effect. They may properly be divided into *sensational*, *perceptional*, and *emotional*.

That the sensational pleasure is distinguishable from the other pleasures which music yields will not be questioned. A sweet sound is agreeable in itself when heard out of relation to other sounds. Tones of various *timbres*, too, are severally appreciated as having their special beauties. Of further elements in the sensational pleasure have to be named those which result from certain congruities between notes and immediately succeeding notes. This pleasure, like the primary pleasure which fine quality yields, appears to have a purely physical basis. We know that the agreeableness of simultaneous tones depends partly on the relative frequency of recurring correspondences of the vibrations producing them, and partly on the relative infrequency of beats, and we may suspect that there is a kindred cause for the agreeableness of successive tones, since the auditory apparatus, which has been at one instant vibrating in a particular manner, will take up certain succeeding vibrations more readily than others. Evidently it is a question of the *degree* of congruity; for the most congruous vibrations, those of the octaves, yield less pleasure when heard in succession than those of which the congruity is not so great. To obtain the greatest pleasure in this and other things there requires both likeness and difference. Recognition of this fact introduces us to the next element of sensational pleasure—that due to contrast; including contrast of pitch, of loudness, and of *timbre.* In this case, as in other cases, the disagreeableness caused by frequent repetition of the same sensation (here literally called "monotony") results from the exhaustion which any single nervous agent undergoes from perpetual stimulation; and contrast gives pleasure because it implies action of an agent which has had rest. It follows that much of the sensational pleasure to be obtained from music depends on such adjustments of sounds as bring into play, without conflict, many nervous elements, exercising all and not over-exerting any. We must not overlook a concomitant effect: with the agreeable sensation is joined a faint emotion of an agreeable kind. Beyond the simple definite pleasure yielded by a sweet tone, there is a vague, diffused pleasure. As indicated in the *Principles of Psychology* (§537), each nervous excitation produces reverberation throughout the nervous system at large; and probably this indefinite emotional pleasure is a consequence. Doubtless some shape is given to it by association. But after observing how much there is in common between the diffused feeling aroused by smelling at a deliciously scented flower and that aroused by listening to a sweet tone, it will, I think, be perceived that the more general cause predominates.

The division between the sensational effects and the perceptional effects is of course indefinite. As above implied, part of the sensational pleasure depends on the relation between each tone and the succeeding tone; and hence this pleasure gradually merges into that which arises from perceiving the structural connexions between the phrases and between the larger parts of musical compositions. Much of the gratification given by a melody consists in the consciousness of the relations between each group of sounds heard and the groups of sounds held in memory as having just passed, as well as those represented as about to come. In many cases the passage listened to would not be regarded as having any beauty were it not for its remembered connexions with passages in the immediate past and the immediate future. If, for example, from the first movement of Beethoven's Funeral-March sonata the first five notes are detached, they appear to be meaningless; but if, the movement being known, they are joined with imaginations of the anticipated phrases, they immediately acquire meaning and beauty. Indefinable as are the causes of this perceptional pleasure in many cases, some causes of it are definable. Symmetry is one. A chief element in melodic effect results from repetitions of phrases which are either identical, or differ only in pitch, or differ only in minor variations; there being in the first case the pleasure derived from perception of complete likeness, and in the other cases the greater pleasure derived from perception of likeness with difference—a perception which is more involved, and therefore exercises a greater number of nervous agents. Next comes, as a source of gratification, the consciousness of pronounced unlikeness or contrast, such as that between passages above the middle tones and passages below, or as that between ascending phrases and descending phrases. And then we rise to larger contrasts; as when, the first theme in a melody having been elaborated, there is introduced another having a certain kinship though in many respects different, after which there is a return to the first theme—a structure which yields more extensive and more complex perceptions of both differences and likenesses. But while perceptional pleasures include much that is of the highest, they also include much that is of the lowest. A certain kind of interest, if not of beauty, is producible by the likenesses and contrasts of musical phrases which are intrinsically meaningless or even ugly. A familiar experience exemplifies this. If a piece of paper is folded and on one side of the crease there is drawn an irregular line in ink, which by closing the paper is blotted on the opposite side of the crease, there results a figure which, in virtue of its symmetry, has some beauty—no matter how entirely without beauty the two lines themselves may be. Similarly, some interest results from the parallelism of musical phrases, notwithstanding utter lack of interest in the phrases themselves. The kind of interest resulting from such parallelisms and from many contrasts, irrespective of any intrinsic worth in their components, is that which is most appreciated by the musically uncultured and gives popularity to miserable drawing-room ballads and vulgar music-hall songs.

The remaining element of musical effect consists in the idealized rendering of emotion. This, as I have sought to show, is the primitive element, and will ever continue to be the vital element; for if " melody is the soul of music," then expression is the soul of melody— the soul without which it is mechanical and meaningless, whatever may be the merit of its form. This primitive element may with tolerable clearness be distinguished from the other elements, and may coexist with them in various degrees—in some cases being the predominant element. Anyone who, in analytical mood, listens to such a song as *Robert, toi qui j'aime*, cannot, I think, fail to perceive that its effectiveness depends on the way in which it exalts and intensifies the traits of passionate utterance. No doubt as music develops, the emotional element (which affects structure chiefly through the forms of phrases) is increasingly complicated with and obscured by the perceptional element, which both modifies these phrases and unites them into symmetrical and contrasted combinations. But though the groups of notes which emotion prompts admit of elaboration into structures that have additional charms due to artfully arranged contrasts and repetitions, the essential element is liable to be thus submerged in the non-essential. Only in melodies of high types, such as the *Addio* of Mozart and *Adelaide* of Beethoven, do we see the two requirements simultaneously fulfilled. Musical genius is shown in achieving the decorative beauty without losing the beauty of emotional meaning.

It goes without saying that there must be otherwise accounted for that relatively modern element in musical effect which has now almost outgrown in importance the other elements—I mean harmony. This cannot be affiliated on the natural language of emotion, since in such language, limited to successive tones, there cannot originate the effects wrought by simultaneous tones. Dependent as harmony is on relations among rates of aerial pulses, its primary basis is purely mechanical; and its secondary basis lies in the compound vibrations which certain combinations of mechanical rhythms cause in the auditory apparatus. The resulting pleasure must therefore be due to nervous excitations of kinds which, by their congruity, exalt one another, and thus generate a larger volume of agreeable sensation. A further pleasure of sensational origin which harmony yields is due to contrapuntal effects. Skilful counterpoint has the general character that it does not repeat in immediate succession similar combinations of tones and similar directions of change; and by thus avoiding temporary over-tax of the nervous structures brought into action, keeps them in better condition for subsequent action. Absence of regard for this requirement characterizes the music of Gluck, of whom Handel said : " He knows no more counterpoint than my cook "; and it is this disregard which produces its cloying character. Respecting the effects of harmony I will add only that the vague emotional accompaniment to the sensation produced by a single sweet tone is paralleled by the stronger emotional accompaniment to the more voluminous and complex sensation produced by a fine chord. Clearly this vague emotion forms a large component in the pleasure which harmony gives.

While thus recognizing, and indeed emphasizing,

the fact that of many traits of developed music my hypothesis respecting the origin of music yields no explanation, let me point out that this hypothesis gains a further general support from its conformity to the law of evolution.   Progressive integration is seen in the immense contrast between the small combinations of tones constituting a cadence of grief, or anger, or triumph, and the vast combinations of tones, simultaneous and successive, constituting an oratorio. Great advance in coherence becomes manifest when from the lax unions among the sounds in which feeling spontaneously expresses itself, or even from those few musical phrases which constitute a simple air, we pass to those elaborate compositions in which portions small and large are tied together into extended organic wholes.   On comparing the unpremeditated inflexions of the voice in emotional speech, vague in tones and times, with those premeditated ones which the musician arranges for stage or concert room, in which the divisions of time are exactly measured, the successive intervals precise, and the harmonies adjusted to a nicety, we observe in the last a far higher definiteness. And immense progress in heterogeneity is seen on putting side by side the monotonous chants of savages with the musical compositions familiar to us ; each of which is relatively heterogeneous within itself, and the assemblage of which forms an immeasurably heterogeneous aggregate.

Strong support for the theory enunciated in this essay, and defended in the foregoing paragraphs, is furnished by the testimonies of two travellers in Hungary, given in works published in 1878 and 1888

H

respectively. Here is an extract from the first of the two:—

> Music is an instinct with these Hungarian gipsies. They play by ear, and with a marvellous precision, not surpassed by musicians who have been subject to the most careful training. . . . The airs they play are most frequently compositions of their own, and are in character quite peculiar. . . . I heard on this occasion one of the gipsy airs which made an indelible impression on my mind; it seemed to me the thrilling utterance of a people's history. There was the low wail of sorrow, of troubled passionate grief, stirring the heart to restlessness, then the sense of turmoil and defeat; but upon this breaks suddenly a wild burst of exultation, of rapturous joy—a triumph achieved, which hurries you along with it in resistless sympathy. The excitable Hungarians can literally become intoxicated with this music— and no wonder. You cannot reason upon it, or explain it, but its strains compel you to sensations of despair and joy, of exultation and excitement, as though under the influence of some potent charm. *Round about the Carpathians*, by Andrew F. Crosse, pp. 11, 12.

Still more graphic and startling is the description given by a more recent traveller, E. Gerard:—

> Devoid of printed notes, the Tzigane is not forced to divide his attention between a sheet of paper and his instrument, and there is consequently nothing to detract from the utter abandonment with which he absorbs himself in his playing. He seems to be sunk in an inner world of his own; the instrument sobs and moans in his hands, and is pressed tight against his

heart as though it had grown and taken root there. This is the true moment of inspiration, to which he rarely gives way, and then only in the privacy of an intimate circle, never before a numerous and unsympathetic audience. Himself spell-bound by the power of the tones he evokes, his head gradually sinking lower and lower over the instrument, the body bent forward in an attitude of rapt attention, and his ear seeming to hearken to far-off ghostly strains audible to himself alone, the untaught Tzigane achieves a perfection of expression unattainable by more professional training.

This power of identification with his music is the real secret of the Tzigane's influence over his audience. Inspired and carried away by his own strains, he must perforce carry his hearers with him as well; and the Hungarian listener throws himself heart and soul into this species of musical intoxication, which to him is the greatest delight on earth. There is a proverb which says, " The Hungarian only requires a gipsy fiddler and a glass of water in order to make him quite drunk "; and, indeed, intoxication is the only word fittingly to describe the state of exultation into which I have seen a Hungarian audience thrown by a gipsy band.

Sometimes, under the combined influence of music and wine, the Tziganes become like creatures possessed; the wild cries and stamps of an equally excited audience only stimulate them to greater exertions. The whole atmosphere seems tossed by billows of passionate harmony; we seem to catch sight of the electric sparks of inspiration flying through the air. It is then that the Tzigane player gives forth everything that is secretly lurking within him—fierce anger, childish wailings, presumptuous exultation, brooding

H 2

melancholy, and passionate despair; and at such moments, as a Hungarian writer has said, one could readily believe in his power of drawing down the angels from heaven into hell!

Listen how another Hungarian has here described the effect of their music: "How it rushes through the veins like electric fire! How it penetrates straight to the soul! In soft plaintive minor tones the *adagio* opens with a slow rhythmical movement: it is a sighing and longing of unsatisfied aspirations; a craving for undiscovered happiness; the lover's yearning for the object of his affection; the expression of mourning for lost joys, for happy days gone for ever; then abruptly changing to a major key, the tones get faster and more agitated; and from the whirlpool of harmony the melody gradually detaches itself, alternately drowned in the foam of overbreaking waves, to reappear floating on the surface with undulating motion—collecting as it were fresh power for a renewed burst of fury. But quickly as the storm came it is gone again, and the music relapses into the melancholy yearnings of heretofore." *The Land beyond the Forest*, vol. II, pp. 122–4. Lond. 1888.

After the evidence thus furnished, argument is almost superfluous. The origin of music as the developed language of emotion seems to be no longer an inference, but simply a description of the fact.

GRACEFULNESS

[*First published in* The Leader *for December* 25, 1852.]

WE do not ascribe gracefulness to cart-horses, tortoises, and hippopotami, in all of which the powers of movement are relatively inferior; but we ascribe it to greyhounds, antelopes, racehorses, all of which have highly efficient locomotive organs. What, then, is this distinctive peculiarity of structure and action which we call Grace?

One night while watching a dancer, and inwardly condemning her *tours de force* as barbarisms which would be hissed were not people such cowards as always to applaud what they think it the fashion to applaud, I remarked that the truly graceful motions occasionally introduced were those performed with comparatively little effort. After calling to mind sundry confirmatory facts, I presently concluded that grace, as applied to motion, describes motion that is effected with economy of force; grace as applied to animal forms describes forms capable of this economy; grace as applied to postures describes postures which may be maintained with this economy; and grace as applied to inanimate objects describes such as exhibit certain analogies to these attitudes and forms.

That this generalization, if not the whole truth, contains at least a large part of it, will, I think, become obvious on considering how habitually we couple the words "easy" and "graceful"; and still more on calling to mind some of the facts on which this sensation is based. The attitude of a soldier drawing himself bolt upright when his serjeant shouts " attention " is more remote from gracefulness than when he relaxes at the words " stand at ease." The *gauche* visitor sitting stiffly on the edge of his chair, and his self-possessed host, whose limbs and body dispose themselves as convenience dictates, are contrasts as much in effort as in elegance. When standing, we commonly economize power by throwing the weight chiefly on one leg, which we straighten to make it serve as a column, while we relax the other; and to the same end we allow the head to lean somewhat on one side. Both these attitudes are imitated in sculpture as elements of grace.

Turning from attitudes to movements, current remarks will be found to imply the same relationship. No one praises, as graceful, a walk that is irregular or jerking, and so displays waste of power; no one sees any beauty in the waddle of a fat man, or the trembling steps of an invalid, in both of which effort is visible. But the style of walking we admire is moderate in velocity, perfectly rhythmical, unaccompanied by violent swinging of the arms, and giving us the impression that there is no conscious exertion, while there is no force thrown away. In dancing, again, the prevailing difficulty—the proper disposal of the arms—well illustrates the same truth. Those who fail in overcoming this difficulty give the spectator the impression that their arms are a trouble to them; they are held stiffly in some meaningless attitude, at an obvious expense of power; they are checked from swinging in the directions in which they would naturally swing; or they are so moved that, instead of helping to maintain the equilibrium, they endanger it. A good dancer, on the contrary, makes us feel that, so far from the arms being in the way, they are of great use. Each motion of them, while it seems naturally to result from a previous motion of the body, is turned to some advantage. We perceive that it has facilitated instead of hindered the general action; or in other words—that an economy of effort has been achieved. Any one wishing to distinctly realize this fact may readily do so by studying the action of the arms in walking. Let him place his arms close to his sides, and there keep them while walking with some rapidity. He will unavoidably fall into a backward and forward motion of the shoulders, of a wriggling, ungraceful character. After persevering in this for a space, until he finds that the action is not only ungraceful but fatiguing, let him allow his arms to swing as usual. The wriggling of the shoulders will cease, the body will move equably forward, and comparative ease will be felt. On analysing this fact he may perceive that the backward motion of each arm is simultaneous with the forward motion of the corresponding leg. If he will attend to his muscular sensations, he will find that this backward swing of the arm is a counterbalance to the forward swing of the leg, and that it is easier to produce this counterbalance by moving the arm than by contorting the body, as he otherwise must do.[1]

[1] A parallel fact further elucidating this is supplied by a locomotive engine. On looking at the driving-wheel there will be found, besides the boss to which the connecting-rod is attached, a corresponding mass of metal on the opposite side of the wheel, and equidistant from the centre; or if the engine

The action of the arms in walking being thus understood, it will be manifest that the graceful employment of them in dancing is simply a complication of the same thing, and that a good dancer is one having so acute a muscular perception as at once to feel in what direction the arms should be moved to counterbalance any motion of the body or legs.

This connexion between gracefulness and economy of force will be most clearly recognized by those who skate. They will remember that all early attempts, and especially the first timid experiments in figure-skating, are alike awkward and fatiguing, and that the acquirement of skill is also the acquirement of ease. The requisite confidence and a due command of the feet having been obtained, those twistings of the trunk and gyrations of the arms, previously used to maintain the balance, are found needless. The body is allowed to follow without control the impulse given to it, the arms to swing where they will; and it is clearly felt that the graceful way of performing any evolution is the way that costs least effort. Spectators can scarcely fail to see the same fact, if they look for it.

be one having inside cylinders, then, on looking between the spokes of the driving-wheel, it will be seen that against each crank is a block of iron similar to it in size but projecting from the axle in the reverse direction. Evidently, being placed on opposite sides of the centre of motion, each crank and its counterbalance move in opposite directions relatively to the axle; and by so doing, neutralize each other's perturbing effects and permit a smooth rotation. This relationship which exists between the motions of the counterbalance and the crank is analogous to that which exists between the motions of the arms and legs in walking; and in the early days of railway-locomotion, before these counterbalance weights were used, locomotive driving-wheels were subject to violent oscillations, analogous to those jerkings of the shoulders which arise when we walk fast without moving our arms.

The reference to skating suggests that graceful motion might be defined as motion in curved lines. Certainly, straight and zig-zag movements are excluded from the conception. The sudden stoppages which angular movements imply are its antithesis; for a leading trait of grace is continuity, flowingness. It will be found, however, that this is merely another aspect of the same truth, and that motion in curved lines is economical motion. Given certain successive positions to be assumed by a limb, then if it be moved in a straight line to the first of these positions, suddenly arrested, and then moved in another direction straight to the second position, and so on, it is clear that, at each arrest, the momentum previously given to the limb must be destroyed at a certain cost of force, and a new momentum given to it at a further cost of force; whereas if, instead of arresting the limb at its first position, its motion be allowed to continue, and a lateral force be impressed to make it diverge towards the second position, a curvilinear motion is the necessary result; and, by making use of the original momentum, force is economized.

If the truth of these conclusions respecting graceful movements be admitted, it cannot, I think, be doubted that graceful form is that kind of form which implies relatively small effort required for self-support, and relatively small effort required for movement. Were it otherwise, there would arise the incongruity that graceful form would either not be associated at all with graceful movement, or that the one would habitually occur in the absence of the other; both which alternatives being at variance with our experience, we must conclude that there exists the relationship indicated. Any one hesitating to admit this will, I think, do so no longer on remembering that the animals which we consider graceful are those so slight in build as not to be burdened by their own weight, and those noted for fleetness and agility; while those we class as ungraceful are those which are alike cumbrous and have the faculty of locomotion but little developed. In the case of the greyhound, especially, we see that the particular modification of the canine type in which economy of weight is the most conspicuous, and in which the facility of muscular motion has been brought to the greatest perfection, is the one which we call most graceful.

How trees and inanimate objects should come to have this epithet applied to them seems less obvious. But remembrance of the fact that we commonly, and perhaps unavoidably, regard all objects under a certain anthropomorphic aspect, will help us to understand it. The stiff branch of an oak tree, standing out at right angles to the trunk, gives us a vague notion of great force expended to keep it in that position; and we call it ungraceful under the same feeling that we call the holding out an arm at right angles to the body ungraceful. Conversely, the lax drooping boughs of a weeping-willow are vaguely associated with limbs in attitudes requiring little effort to maintain them, and the term " graceful," by which we describe these, we apply by metaphor to the boughs of the willow.

I may as well here venture the hypothesis that the idea of Grace as displayed by other beings has its subjective basis in Sympathy. The same faculty which makes us shudder on seeing another in danger— which sometimes causes motions of our own limbs on seeing another struggle or fall, gives us a vague participation in all the muscular sensations which those around us are experiencing. When their motions are violent or awkward, we feel in a slight degree the disagreeable sensations which we should have were they our own. When they are easy, we sympathize with the pleasant sensations they imply in those exhibiting them.

USE AND BEAUTY

[*First published in* The Leader *for January* 3, 1852.]

IN one of his essays Emerson remarks that what Nature at one time provides for use, she afterwards turns to ornament; and he cites in illustration the structure of a sea-shell, in which the parts that have for a while formed the mouth are at the next season of growth left behind, and become decorative nodes and spines.

Ignoring the implied teleology, which does not here concern us, it has often occurred to me that this same remark might be extended to the progress of Humanity. Here, too, the appliances of one era serve as embellishments to the next. Equally in institutions, creeds, customs, and superstitions, we may trace this evolution of beauty out of what was once purely utilitarian.

The contrast between the feeling with which we regard portions of the Earth's surface still left in their original state, and the feeling with which the savage regarded them, is an instance that comes first in order of time. If any one walking over Hampstead Heath will note how strongly its picturesqueness is brought out by contrast with the surrounding cultivated fields and the masses of houses lying in the distance, and will further reflect that, had this irregular gorse-covered surface extended on all sides to the horizon, it would have looked dreary and prosaic rather than pleasing, he will see that to the primitive man a country so clothed presented no beauty at all. To him it was merely a haunt of wild animals, and a ground out of which roots might be dug. What have become for us places of relaxation and enjoyment—places for afternoon strolls and for gathering flowers—were his places for labour and food, probably arousing in his mind none but utilitarian associations.

Ruined castles afford obvious instances of this metamorphosis of the useful into the beautiful. To feudal barons and their retainers, security was the chief, if not the only end, sought in choosing the sites and styles of their strongholds. Probably they aimed as little at the picturesque as do the builders of cheap brick houses in our modern towns. Yet what were erected for shelter and safety, and what in those early days fulfilled an important function in the social economy, have now assumed a purely ornamental character. They serve as scenes for picnics; pictures of them decorate our drawing-rooms; and each supplies its surrounding districts with legends for Christmas Eve.

On following out the train of thought suggested by this last illustration, we may see that not only do the material exuviæ of past social states become the ornaments of our landscapes, but that past habits, manners, and arrangements serve as ornamental elements in our literature. The tyrannies which, to the serfs who bore them, were harsh and dreary facts; the feuds which, to those who took part in them, were very practical life-and-death affairs; the mailed, moated, sentinelled security which was irksome to the nobles who needed it; the imprisonments, and tortures, and escapes, which were stern and quite prosaic realities to all concerned in them; have become to us material for romantic tales—material which, when woven into Ivanhoes and Marmions, serves for amusement in leisure hours, and becomes poetical by contrast with our daily lives.

Thus also is it with extinct creeds. Stonehenge, which in the hands of the Druids had a governmental influence over men, is in our day a place for antiquarian excursions, and its attendant priests are worked up into an opera. Greek sculptures, preserved for their beauty in our galleries of art, and copied for the decoration of pleasure grounds and entrance halls, once lived in men's minds as gods demanding obedience; as did also the grotesque idols that now amuse the visitors to our museums.

Equally marked is this change of function in the case of minor superstitions. The fairy lore, which in past times was matter of grave belief, and held sway over people's conduct, has since been transformed into ornament for *A Midsummer Night's Dream*, *The Tempest*, *The Fairy Queen*, and endless small tales and poems, and still affords subjects for children's story-books, themes for ballets, and plots for Planché's burlesques. Gnomes, and genii, and afrits, losing their terrors, give piquancy to the woodcuts in our illustrated editions of the *Arabian Nights*. While ghost-stories, and tales of magic and witchcraft, after serving to amuse boys and girls in their leisure hours, become matter for jocose allusions that enliven tea-table conversation.

Even our serious literature and our speeches are relieved by ornaments drawn from such sources. A Greek myth is often used as a parallel by which to vary the monotony of some grave argument. The lecturer breaks the dead level of his practical discourse by illustrations drawn from bygone customs, events, or beliefs. And metaphors, similarly derived, give brilliancy to political orations, and to *Times* leading articles.

Indeed, on careful inquiry, I think it will be found that we turn to purposes of beauty most bygone phenomena which are at all conspicuous. The busts of great men in our libraries, and their tombs in our churches; the once useful but now purely ornamental heraldic symbols; the monks, nuns, and convents, which give interest to a certain class of novels; the bronze medieval soldiers used for embellishing drawing-rooms; the gilt apollos which recline on timepieces; the narratives that serve as plots for our great dramas; and the events that afford subjects for historical pictures—these and such like illustrations of the metamorphosis of the useful into the beautiful are so numerous as to suggest that, did we search diligently enough, we should find that in some place, or under some circumstance, nearly every notable product of the past has assumed a decorative character.

And here the mention of historical pictures reminds me that an inference may be drawn from all this, bearing directly on the practice of art. It has of late years been a frequent criticism upon our historical painters that they err in choosing their subjects from the past, and that, would they found a genuine and vital school, they must render on canvas the life and deeds and aims of our own time. If, however, there be any significance in the foregoing facts, it seems doubtful whether this criticism is a just one. For if it be the course of things that what has performed some active function in society during one era becomes available for ornament in a subsequent one, it almost follows that, conversely, whatever is performing some active function now, or has very recently performed one, does not possess the ornamental character, and is consequently inapplicable to any purpose of which beauty is the aim, or of which it is a needful ingredient.

Still more reasonable will this conclusion appear when we consider the nature of this process by which the useful is changed into the ornamental. An essential prerequisite to all beauty is *contrast*. To obtain artistic effect, light must be put in juxtaposition with shade, bright colours with dull colours, a fretted surface with a plain one. *Forte* passages in music must have *piano* passages to relieve them; concerted pieces need interspersing with solos; and rich chords must not be continuously repeated. In the drama we demand contrast of characters, of scenes, of sentiment, of style. In prose composition an eloquent passage should have a comparatively plain setting, and in poems great effect is obtained by occasional change of versification. This general principle will, I think, explain the transformation of the bygone useful into the present beautiful. It is by virtue of their contrast with our present modes of life that past modes of life look interesting and romantic. Just as a picnic, which is a temporary return to an aboriginal condition, derives, from its unfamiliarity, a certain poetry which it would not have were it habitual; so everything ancient gains, from its relative novelty to us, an element of interest. Gradually as, by the growth of society, we leave behind the customs, manners, arrangements, and all the products, material and mental, of a bygone age—gradually as we recede from these so far that there arises a conspicuous difference between them and those we are familiar with; so gradually do they begin to assume to us a poetical aspect, and become applicable for ornament. And hence it follows that things and events which are close to us, and which are accompanied by associations of ideas not markedly contrasted with our ordinary associations, are *relatively* inappropriate for purposes of art. I say relatively because an incident of modern life or even of daily life may acquire adequate fitness for art purposes by an unusualness of some other kind than that due to unlikeness between past and present.

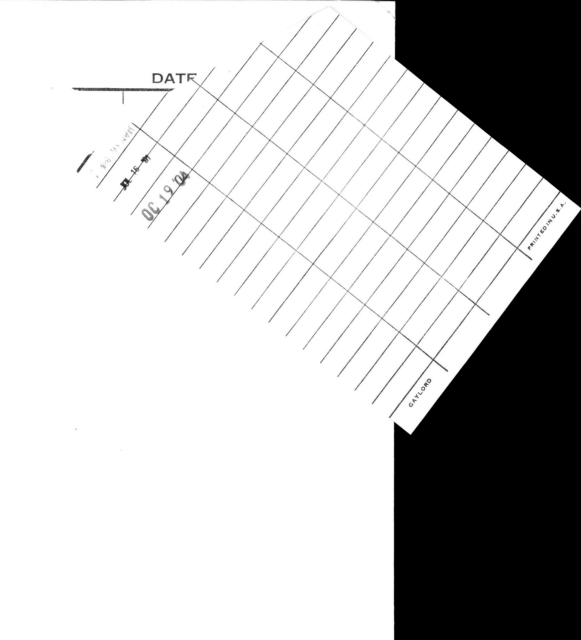

DATE

OC 19 '04